UNCTAD/ITCD/TSB/2003/1

The African Growth and Opportunity Act: A Preliminary Assessment

A report prepared for the United Nations Conference on Trade and Development

UNITED NATIONS
New York and Geneva, April 2003

Note

The descriptions and classification of countries and territories in this report and the arrangement of material do not imply the expression of any opinion whatsoever on the part of the Secretariat of the United Nations concerning the legal status of any country, territory, city or area, or of its authorities, or concerning the delimitation of its frontiers or boundaries, or regarding its economic system or degree of development.

UNCTAD/ITCD/TSB/2003/1

UN 2
TD/UNCTAD/ITCD/TSB/2003/1

UNITED NATIONS PUBLICATION
Sales No. E.03.II.D.15
ISBN 92-1-112587-1

iii

Contents

Tables

Figures

Appendix

Acknowledgement

This report was prepared by Mr. Craig VanGrasstek, President, VanGrasstek Communications, Washington, DC. The opinions expressed in it are those of the author and do not necessarily reflect the views of the UNCTAD secretariat.

1

Introduction

The African Growth and Opportunity Act (AGOA) was enacted into law as part of the Trade and Development Act of 2000 (Public Law 106-200). It is the latest in a series of regional initiatives in United States trade policy that are based on the general philosophy of "trade, not aid" as the chief tool for promoting economic development. The intention is to offer trade preferences to the beneficiary countries as a complement to foreign aid, and encourage them to adopt reforms in their economic, investment and trade policies. The most immediate benefit that it extends to sub-Saharan African countries is expanded product coverage under the Generalized System of Preferences (GSP), as well as tariff- and quota-free exports of textile and apparel products to the United States. The programme also contemplates the future negotiation of a free trade agreement (FTA) between the United States and those countries, which would entail the exchange of reciprocal commitments rather than the one-way preferences of AGOA, but not extend to the President the authority to negotiate such an arrangement. Other provisions establish a higher priority for the region in US foreign economic policy agencies, provide for closer coordination between the United States and African countries, and increase aid and technical assistance.

AGOA has now been in place long enough for a very preliminary assessment of its impact to be undertaken. President Clinton designated the first countries under the programme in October 2000, and then designated products for AGOA treatment that December; the first shipments of duty-free goods entered the United States in January 2001. While it may take several years before sufficient data are available to conduct a comprehensive review of the programme's duty- and quota-free treatment for the beneficiary countries, we now have enough information to make provisional judgements.

Two US government agencies have already offered preliminary assessments of AGOA's impact. The AGOA statute requires that the President submit to Congress a comprehensive annual report on the operation of the programme. This report is the responsibility of the Office of the United States Trade Representative (USTR), which asked in 2000 that the United States International Trade Commission (USITC) produce annual reports for five years on this topic. The USITC issued its second annual report in December 2001,[1] while the USTR issued its most recent AGOA report in May 2002.[2] Both of these reports offer a wealth of information on specific steps taken to implement the programme, as well as data on the trade flows over the past few years. However, they do not necessarily exhaust the analytical possibilities. The USTR report is issued by an agency that is charged with both promoting and implementing the initiative, a point that may explain the "spin" it gives to some facts.[3] The USITC report provides a great deal of data on tariff rates and trade flows, but reaches no firm conclusions regarding the relationship between them.

---

[1] *US Trade and Investment with Sub-Saharan Africa — Second Annual Report,* USITC Publication 3476 (Washington, DC: USITC, 2001).

[2] *2002 Comprehensive Report on US Trade and Investment Policy Toward Sub-Saharan Africa and Implementation of the African Growth and Opportunity Act* (Washington, DC: USTR, 2002), hereinafter cited as "USTR, *2002 AGOA Report*".

[3] For example, the first empirical observation in the report is that "US imports from sub-Saharan Africa have increased 61.5 percent over the last two years" (p. 1). While true, this statement glosses over the fact (noted 23 pages later) that these imports declined by 9.3 per cent during 2001. Neither the increase in 1999–2000 nor the decrease in 2000–2001 should be attributed *post hoc ergo propter hoc* to AGOA.

The purpose of the present report is to offer an early assessment of the utility of the AGOA tariff preferences as an instrument of special and differential (S&D) treatment for the beneficiary countries. The objective here is neither to praise nor to condemn AGOA, but instead to reach quantifiable conclusions regarding its actual utility for the exporting countries. The report does so first by examining the general trends in the S&D treatment that the United States extends to developing countries, and then by placing AGOA in this broader context. The overall thesis of this analysis can be summarized as follows: tariff preferences in general offer a relatively small and declining margin of preference to developing countries, and the additional benefits of the AGOA preferences represent a modest expansion over the preferential treatment that sub-Saharan countries already enjoyed under the GSP. There are exceptions to this general rule, both for specific countries and for products, but the general pattern is clear. Apart from the textile and apparel sector, where substantial trade barriers imply equally substantial margins of preference for AGOA beneficiary countries, the programme's duty-free benefits appear to offer only a slight improvement over the status quo for most African exports. That point is especially true for those countries that have already enjoyed duty-free access to the US market for virtually all of their non-textile exports. Even in the case of textile and apparel exports, the global quota regime suggests that the benefits extended under AGOA are time-bound.

These observations suggest that the non-tariff aspects of the programme may ultimately be much more important to the beneficiary countries than are the tariff preferences per se. Those features of the AGOA fall outside the scope of the present analysis. For further information on the technical assistance and other measures that various agencies of the US Government are providing to promote reform in sub-Saharan African countries, see the USTR report.[4]

The place of special and differential treatment in US trade policy

AGOA does not extend wholly new or unique benefits to sub-Saharan African countries. On the contrary, it is only the latest in a series of preferential arrangements with specific regions of the developing world. As can be appreciated from the data in table 1, the US trade regime today is a patchwork quilt of special programmes and agreements, in which those countries that receive only "normal trade relations" (NTR) account for just over half of all US imports.[5] Most sub-Saharan African countries were already designated for benefits under the GSP when AGOA came into being, and many of them also enjoyed the broader product coverage that is available to LDCs.[6] The real benefits of the programme thus need to be compared with the status of countries in US policy prior to AGOA. The difference between AGOA status and ordinary NTR treatment may appear rather wide, but the more appropriate comparison is between AGOA and GSP (either in its ordinary or LDC versions).

---

[4] See especially sections V ("Trade Capacity Building") and VI ("Technical Assistance and Other AGOA-Related Initiatives") in USTR, *2002 AGOA Report*.

[5] In current US law and practice, the term "most favoured nation" (MFN) has been replaced by "normal trade relations." This change was made by law in 1998. From a practical perspective, there is no difference between NTR and MFN. While "MFN" is the more appropriate term in WTO usage, we use "NTR" in most of this paper because this is primarily an examination of US law and policy.

[6] The pre-AGOA status of specific countries under the GSP is set out in table 4.

Table 1
The hierarchy of preferences in the US trade regime

Listed in declining order of preference; shares of 2001 imports from a total of $1,132.6 billion

		Share of total US imports	Average tariff on imports	Share enjoying preferences
Reciprocal preferences				
Free trade Agreements (FTA)	Canada, Israel, Jordan and Mexico enjoy comprehensive duty-free access	31.7%	0.1%	54.8%
Non-reciprocal regional preferences				
African Growth and Opportunity Act (AGOA)	Sub-Saharan African countries enjoy duty-free access for nearly all goods; some also have duty- and quota-free access for textiles and apparel	0.8%	0.7%	46.6%
Caribbean Basin Initiative (CBI)	Central America and Caribbean countries enjoy duty-free for most goods, and "NAFTA parity" for all others	1.8%	2.8%	41.1%
Andean Trade Preferences Act (ATPA)	Four Andean countries enjoy duty-free access for most goods (this expired in late 2001 but may be renewed soon)	0.8%	1.5%	19.4%
Non-reciprocal global preferences				
Generalized System of Preferences (GSP)	Beneficiaries enjoy duty-free access for some goods, but many items are excluded; product coverage is wider for the least developed countries	9.8%	3.6%	14.1%
Non-preferential treatment				
Normal trade relations (NTR)	Formerly known as most favoured nation (MFN); NTR for some Communist or transitional economies is conditional upon their emigration practices	53.9%	2.2%	0.0%
Denied NTR	Cuba, the Lao People's Democratic Republic and the Democratic People's Republic of Korea are subject to non-NTR rates	<0.1%	35.1%	0.0%
Trade embargo	Iraq and the Islamic Republic of Iran receive NTR treatment but are subject to partial trade embargoes	0.4%	0.3%	0.0%
World		100.0%	1.6%	22.1%

Note: Except for countries that are subject to trade embargoes, imports from a country are counted in the category representing the most favourable treatment that it receives. For example, imports from AGOA, ATPA and CBI countries are classified here under those programmes even though they are also eligible for GSP treatment.

Source: Classifications from the Harmonized Tariff Schedule of the United States (2002). Trade data calculated from the USITC's trade database.

AGOA is in the second tier of preferential treatment, below free trade agreements but above the GSP. Its main shortcomings vis-à-vis an FTA is that there are a few products that AGOA does not cover and the benefits are not permanent. AGOA is one of three regional preferential programmes that are more generous than the GSP, insofar as they each cover a wider range of products than the GSP and are not restricted by that programme's limitations (e.g. "competitive need" limits on specific products from specific countries). AGOA appears to be the most comprehensive of the three regional programmes in its actual utilization. A higher share of imports from AGOA countries entered the United States on a preferential basis in 2001 than did imports from the beneficiary countries of the Caribbean Basin and Andean programmes, and the average tariff rate on total US imports from AGOA countries was below 1 per cent.

The figures in table 1 give only the grossest data about the actual use of these programmes, and do not tell us whether they stimulate any additional trade between the United States and the beneficiary countries. We do not yet have enough time-series data on US imports under AGOA to reach definitive conclusions on this point, but the experiences with other preferential agreements and programmes offer useful guidance. As shown in table 2, the data do not support a strong link between preferences and export performance. The table summarizes the changes in US imports of non-oil,[7] non-apparel[8] products from major partners during 1991–2001. If preferential tariff treatment were a major determinant of success in export competition, we would expect to find a tight correlation between the degree of preferences and the rate of growth in exports. The data show no such pattern. While both Canada and Mexico enjoyed nearly complete duty-free access to the US market during this period, the growth in Canada's exports to the US market was below the world average, while Mexico was well above. Among developing countries, one would expect the beneficiaries of the Caribbean Basin Initiative (CBI) and the Andean Trade Preferences Act (ATPA) to do much better than countries that enjoy the much less generous benefits of the GSP; the same should be true for the beneficiaries of the special GSP programme for LDCs. Quite to the contrary, however, imports from the CBI, ATPA and LDC countries grew at a much slower rate than imports from the world as a whole, while the ordinary GSP beneficiary countries slightly outperformed the world average. And how can one explain the wide range of experience among the countries enjoying no preferences at all? Japan greatly underperformed the global average, the European Union approximated it and China beat it by a vast margin. That observation is especially troublesome when one considers that China exports more high-tariff goods such as textiles and footwear than do Japan and the European Union; if tariff rates determined export performance, China should have performed poorly by comparison with Japan and the European Union.

The only conclusion that one can reliably draw from table 2 is that countries' performances in exports to the United States over the past decade were not determined by the tariff treatment that they received. The data instead hint at a more intriguing possibility: export performance correlates with economic reforms in the exporting country. In North America, for example, Mexico has undergone much more significant reforms over the past decade than has Canada. This has helped to stimulate foreign investment and trade. The same pattern is discernible among countries that have only NTR access to the US market. China has made significant progress towards a market-oriented

---

[7] The table excludes data on crude oil and natural gas in order to eliminate a major source of price volatility. Note also that the US tariffs on these products are very low, and so the potential benefits of preferential treatment are slight.

[8] Apparel trade is summarized in table 3.

economy over the last decade, and its exports to the United States have soared. The European Union underwent no major changes, and its exports grew at a normal pace while Japan stagnated, as did its exports. Proving or disproving a linkage between reforms and export performance is a task well outside the scope of this study, but the suggested pattern is nonetheless interesting.

Table 2
US imports of non-oil, non-apparel products from selected partners by tariff treatment of the exporting country or group, 1991–2001

Millions of current dollars, imports for consumption, customs value

	1991	2001	Increase	Departure from norm
Full duty-free access*				
Canada	82,950	187,961	126.6%	-13.2
Mexico	24,507	113,329	362.4%	+222.6
Substantial duty-free access				
CBI beneficiary countries	5,148	10,290	99.9%	-39.9
ATPA beneficiary countries	3,405	6,943	103.9%	-35.9
LDC GSP beneficiary countries	757	1,010	33.4%	-106.4
Limited duty-free access				
GSP beneficiary countries**	35,313	86,921	146.1%	+6.3
No duty-free access				
European Union	89,084	214,748	141.1%	+1.3
Japan	90,986	125,986	38.5%	-101.3
China	14,200	92,029	548.1%	+408.3
World	413,960	992,786	139.8%	—

* Canada's duty-free treatment was phased in during 1989–1998; Mexico's phase-in began in 1994 and is still under way.
** This category excludes data for those GSP beneficiary countries listed in the CBI, ATPA or LDC GSP categories.

Note: The data exclude all items in SIC categories 13 (natural gas and crude oil) and 23 (apparel and related items).
Source: Calculated from USITC data.

The observations in table 2 come as no surprise when one considers the inherent limitations of tariff preferences. As a general rule, we would expect the power of a preferential programme to be proportional to the magnitude of the protective barriers that it overcomes. A programme that allows countries to bypass a high tariff wall should thus be very helpful. Conversely, tariff preferences will not be very effective when average rates of duty are relatively low and declining. As was shown in table 1, the average US tariff rate on all imports in 2001 was a mere 1.6 per cent. Even when one focuses solely on imports from countries that receive NTR treatment without any form of preferences, the average tariff was only 2.2 per cent. This suggests that, on average, the margins of preference extended by these programmes will be modest. That point is doubly true for the GSP, insofar as that programme excludes many of the sectors that are subject to relatively high NTR tariff rates (notably textiles, apparel and footwear).

Table 3
US imports of apparel products from selected partners by tariff and quota treatment of the exporting country or group, 1991–2001

Millions of current dollars, imports for consumption, customs value

	1991	2001	Increase	Departure from norm
Duty-free & quota-free access				
Canada	377	1,960	419.9%	+274.6
Mexico	1,487	9,021	506.7%	+361.4
Dutiable but quota-free access				
CBI beneficiary countries	2,548	9,374	267.9%	+122.6
Dutiable & subject to quota				
China	4,099	9,951	142.8%	-2.5
Hong Kong (China)	4,015	4,312	7.4%	-137.9
Rep. of Korea	2,800	2,244	-19.9%	-165.2
World	27,376	67,160	145.3%	—

Source: Calculated from USITC data.

While tariff preferences are generally limited, preferential quota treatment can extend substantial benefits. Economic theory holds that *ceteris paribus* quotas are more restrictive than tariffs. This naturally implies that preferential quota treatment will be a much more effective form of S&D treatment than preferential tariff treatment. The data in table 3 offer strong support for the contention that preferential quota treatment is indeed beneficial. Over the period 1991–2001, total US imports of apparel products increased by 145.3 per cent. The rate of increase was about three times greater for the North American Free Trade Agreement (NAFTA) partners, a fact that can be attributed to the combined quota and tariff preferences that they enjoyed. During most of this period the CBI beneficiary countries enjoyed quota but not tariff preferences.[9] Their rate of growth was not as impressive as that of the NAFTA countries, but was nevertheless almost twice as high as the global average. The largest suppliers of these products to the United States, most notably China, found their export growth impeded by the quotas.

These observations suggest that AGOA's duty- and quota-free treatment for textile and apparel imports could be very beneficial. However, even this favourable conclusion must be qualified in three important respects. First, relief from quota restrictions does not represent a change in the status quo for most sub-Saharan African countries.[10] There had been a hypothetical possibility that quotas might be imposed on textile and apparel imports from other countries in the region, but prior to

---

[9] Starting in 2001, these countries have also enjoyed "NAFTA parity" in the application of US tariffs on textile and apparel products.

[10] In 1997 the USITC estimated that quota-free treatment would not have a very significant impact, given the fact that only two countries were then subject to quotas. It found that US imports of apparel from the region would increase between 0.4 and 0.6 per cent. It further calculated that if both quotas and tariffs on US imports of apparel were eliminated, imports of apparel from the region would increase by 26.4 to 45.9 per cent. Imports of duty- and quota-free textiles would increase by 10.5–16.8 per cent. USIC, *Likely Impact of Providing Quota-Free and Duty-Free Entry to Textiles and Apparel from Sub-Saharan Africa,* USITC Publication 3056 (Washington, DC: USITC, 1997), pp. 3–10.

AGOA only Kenya and Mauritius were subject to such restrictions. Second, the value of quota-free treatment will disappear when there are no more quotas. The Multifibre Arrangement quota regime is scheduled to vanish altogether by the year 2005,[11] after which time the only protection in major import markets will be tariffs and the contingent measures of trade-remedy laws (e.g. safeguards and anti-dumping duties). This means that the prospects for preferential quota treatment are evaporating as well. After 2005, AGOA beneficiaries will still enjoy tariff preferences but will be on a "level playing field" as far as quotas are concerned. It is possible that after 2005 there will be a major consolidation of the global textile and apparel industry. Even preferential tariff treatment may not offer sufficient preferential advantages to ensure the export competitiveness and economic survival of some producers. Third, the preferences that AGOA countries enjoy are conditional upon their meeting strict rules of origin. The significance of this last point is explored in greater depth later in this analysis.

Implementation of AGOA

AGOA has the potential to eliminate all duties on all products that the United States imports from all sub-Saharan African countries. Viewed in the abstract, the benefits of the AGOA may sound extremely generous. The available data nevertheless suggest that, for most countries in the region, the net impact is likely to be small for non-textile products. That was certainly the experience of US trading partners in the Caribbean Basin and the Andean countries. Policy makers in these regions were disappointed after the CBI and ATPA programmes had been in effect for a few years but failed to produce major increases in US imports. Their disappointment should have been tempered by a more informed appreciation of the limited margins of preference that can be had in an environment of generally low trade barriers. Sub-Saharan African countries would be well advised to bear this same point in mind when assessing the probable effects of AGOA. The actual benefits of the programme will vary by both country and product, as discussed below, but as a general rule the beneficiaries should not expect this programme to represent a vast improvement in the terms of their access to the US market.

The designation of products

Although the programme contemplates the extension of duty-free treatment to virtually all products that do not currently receive open access to the US market, there is one important qualification. The law permits the President to designate to AGOA only those products that are determined not to be "import-sensitive in the context of imports from beneficiary sub-Saharan African countries". Following reviews by the USTR and the USITC, President Clinton proclaimed the list of AGOA-eligible products in December 2000.[12] The proclamation provided AGOA treatment for 1,835 items, which represented an apparently considerable increase over the 4,650 products that were already eligible for duty-free treatment under the GSP.[13]

The results of the product-designation process can be seen in either a positive or a negative light.

---

[11] The terms of China's accession to the WTO call for the quotas on its textile and apparel products to be phased out over a longer period.

[12] Proclamation 7388 of 18 December 2000, "To Modify Duty-Free Treatment under the Generalized System of Preferences for Sub-Saharan African Countries and for Other Purposes", *Federal Register,* Vol. 65, No. 246 (21 December 2000), pp. 80723–80732.

[13] USTR, *2002 AGOA Report*, p. 16.

The good news is that this review eliminated almost no products of interest to AGOA countries. When one looks product by product at the leading imports from all 48 of the potential beneficiary countries, there is only one product currently imported from one country that is not eligible for duty-free treatment: refined sugar from Swaziland. This item accounted for a negligible share of US imports from that country in 2001.[14] The bad news is that the net result of the process is not significantly different from the treatment extended to LDCs under the GSP. Except for textile and apparel products, virtually all dutiable items that the United States currently imports from sub-Saharan LDCs were already eligible for duty-free treatment under the GSP. In fact, among the leading imports from sub-Saharan African countries in 2001 there was only one item newly designated for the AGOA that would not have been eligible for duty-free GSP treatment when imported from an LDC: certain watches imported from the Republic of the Congo.[15] This means that little scope was left for additional preferences under AGOA for 30 out of the 48 countries eligible for designation to AGOA. Conversely, the programme is potentially much more significant for the 18 non-LDC countries in the region.

The designation of countries

AGOA benefits are not automatically extended to all the countries that are eligible. AGOA establishes a series of eligibility criteria that countries must meet for designation to the programme, and also provides for the removal of countries that are later found to be not in compliance with the requirements. The decision on the designation of individual countries is the responsibility of the President, advised in this task by the USTR and the inter-agency Trade Policy Staff Committee. Two of the eligibility criteria are stated in a negative fashion, requiring that a country not "engage in activities that undermine United States national security or foreign policy interests" or "engage in gross violations of internationally recognized human rights or provide support for acts of international terrorism and cooperat[e] in international efforts to eliminate human rights violations and terrorist activities". On a more positive note, designation is conditional upon findings that a country "has established, or is making continual progress toward establishing" such things as "a market-based economy," "the rule of law" and "the elimination of barriers to United States trade and investment".

President Clinton issued a proclamation on 2 October 2000 designating 34 out of 48 sub-Saharan African countries as beneficiary countries under AGOA.[16] President Bush later designated two other countries — Côte d'Ivoire and Swaziland — in 2002. These designations were made only after countries were found to be in compliance with the designation requirements for the programme, which in some cases meant obtaining commitments by which countries agreed to make changes in their economic or political practices.[17] One fourth of the four dozen potential AGOA beneficiaries have not yet been designated for the programme. Three of them made no such request, and the remaining nine countries were denied. The denials were variously based on findings related to

---

[14] See table A-43 in the appendix to this report.

[15] See table A-12 in the appendix to this report.

[16] Proclamation 7350 of 2 October 2000, "To Implement the African Growth and Opportunity Act and to Designate Eritrea as a Beneficiary Developing Country for Purposes of the Generalized System of Preferences", *Federal Register* Vol. 65, No. 193 (4 October 2000), pp. 59319–59327.

[17] See USTR, *2002 AGOA Report*, pages 34-36.

economic reforms, the rule of law, protection of human rights, labour rights, corruption, and other matters.[18]

The status of countries under the programme, together with their prior status under the GSP, is summarized in table 4. The table also distinguishes between "partial" and "full" AGOA benefits. "Full" benefits are limited to those countries that have been certified as eligible for the programme's textile and apparel treatment. Benefits in this sector are available only if the country (a) adopts an efficient visa system to guard against unlawful trans-shipment of such goods and the use of counterfeit documents; and (b) enacts legislation or promulgates regulations that would permit US Customs verification teams to have the access necessary to investigate allegations of trans-shipment through the country. The law directs the President to deny benefits to any exporter that has engaged in trans-shipment with respect to textile or apparel products from a beneficiary sub-Saharan African country, and includes other enforcement provisions as well.[19] Twelve countries completed the process of obtaining certification for textile and apparel benefits in 2001, and another five achieved this status in 2002.[20] Just over half of the 36 AGOA-designated countries are still limited to partial benefits under the programme.

Initial and potential results of the AGOA

If one were to use the crudest measure of preferential treatment, AGOA benefits would appear to be quite large. As shown in figure 1, the percentage of imports from AGOA countries that entered the United States on a preferential basis has risen dramatically since the preferences entered into force. During the 1990s, less than 10 per cent of US imports from the 36 countries — and sometimes substantially less than 10 per cent — entered duty-free under the GSP. The share rose to 46.6 per cent in 2001, and to 58.6 per cent in the first quarter of 2002. This is a deceptively simple measure, however, and can be attributed in large measure to the preferential treatment that is now extended to imports of low-tariff energy products from a handful of countries in the region. The United States imported $7.6 billion worth of goods under AGOA in 2001, of which $3.7 billion was liquid natural gas, $2.8 billion was crude oil and $271.5 million was refined petroleum products. All other products accounted for less than 10 per cent of the total.[21] Oil is subject to a low tariff of either 5.25¢ or 10.5¢ per barrel, which amount to about 0.2–0.4 per cent *ad valorem* at recent prices. The preponderance of energy products in US imports from the region greatly distorts all averages.

---

[18] For the rationale behind each of the denials see the relevant country sections in USTR, *2002 AGOA Report*.

[19] The law directs the Customs Service to monitor, and report annually to Congress, on the effectiveness of certain anti-circumvention systems and on measures taken by sub-Saharan African countries that export textiles or apparel to the United States to prevent circumvention. It also authorizes the President to impose appropriate remedies, including restrictions on or the removal of quota-free and duty-free treatment, in the event that textile and apparel articles from a beneficiary sub-Saharan African country are being imported in such increased quantities as to cause serious damage (or actual threat thereof) to the domestic industry producing like or directly competitive articles.

[20] For further information on this aspect of the programme, see US Customs Service, *What Every Member of the Trade Community Should Know About: The African Growth and Opportunity Act* (Washington, DC: USCS, 2001). See also USTR, *2002 AGOA Report*, pp. 17–21.

[21] These numbers are calculated from USITC data.

Table 4
Past status and current status of sub-Saharan African countries under AGOA

Country	Prior GSP status	AGOA designation	Textile certification
LDCs not designated for AGOA benefits			
Angola	LDC beneficiary country	Not designated	Not certified
Burundi	LDC beneficiary country	Not designated	Not certified
Burkina Faso	LDC beneficiary country	Not designated	Not certified
Comoros*	LDC beneficiary country	Not designated	Not certified
Dem. Rep. of the Congo	LDC beneficiary country	Not designated	Not certified
Equatorial Guinea	LDC beneficiary country	Not designated	Not certified
Gambia	LDC beneficiary country	Not designated	Not certified
Somalia*	LDC beneficiary country	Not designated	Not certified
Togo	LDC beneficiary country	Not designated	Not certified
LDCs with partial AGOA benefits			
Benin	LDC beneficiary country	2 October 2000	Not certified
Cape Verde	LDC beneficiary country	2 October 2000	Not certified
Central African Rep.	LDC beneficiary country	2 October 2000	Not certified
Chad	LDC beneficiary country	2 October 2000	Not certified
Republic of the Congo	LDC beneficiary country	2 October 2000	Not certified
Djibouti	LDC beneficiary country	2 October 2000	Not certified
Guinea	LDC beneficiary country	2 October 2000	Not certified
Guinea-Bissau	LDC beneficiary country	2 October 2000	Not certified
Mali	LDC beneficiary country	2 October 2000	Not certified
Niger	LDC beneficiary country	2 October 2000	Not certified
Rwanda	LDC beneficiary country	2 October 2000	Not certified
Sao Tome & Principe	LDC beneficiary country	2 October 2000	Not certified
Sierra Leone**	LDC beneficiary country	2 October 2000	Not certified
LDCs with full AGOA benefits			
Ethiopia	LDC beneficiary country	2 October 2000	2 August 2001
Lesotho	LDC beneficiary country	2 October 2000	23 April 2001
Madagascar	LDC beneficiary country	2 October 2000	6 March 2001
Malawi	LDC beneficiary country	2 October 2000	15 August 2001
Mozambique	LDC beneficiary country	2 October 2000	6 February 2002
United Rep. of Tanzania	LDC beneficiary country	2 October 2000	4 February 2002
Uganda	LDC beneficiary country	2 October 2000	23 October 2001
Zambia	LDC beneficiary country	2 October 2000	17 December 2001

Continued next page

Country	Prior GSP status	AGOA designation	Textile certification
GSP beneficiaries not designated for AGOA benefits			
Zimbabwe	Beneficiary country	Not designated	Not certified
GSP beneficiaries with partial AGOA benefits			
Côte d'Ivoire	Beneficiary country	16 May 2002	Not certified
Seychelles	Beneficiary country	2 October 2000	Not certified
GSP beneficiaries with full AGOA benefits			
Botswana	Beneficiary country	2 October 2000	27 August 2001
Cameroon	Beneficiary country	2 October 2000	1 March 2002
Ghana	Beneficiary country	2 October 2000	20 March 2002
Kenya	Beneficiary country	2 October 2000	18 January 2001
Mauritius	Beneficiary country	2 October 2000	19 January 2001
Namibia	Beneficiary country	2 October 2000	3 December 2001
Senegal	Beneficiary country	2 October 2000	23 April 2002
South Africa	Beneficiary country	2 October 2000	7 March 2001
Swaziland	Beneficiary country	17 January 2002	26 July 2001
Non-GSP beneficiaries not designated for AGOA benefits			
Liberia	Not designated	Not designated	Not certified
Sudan*	Not designated	Not designated	Not certified
Non-GSP beneficiaries with partial AGOA benefits*			
Eritrea	Designated in 2000	2 October 2000	Not certified
Gabon	Designated in 1999	2 October 2000	Not certified
Mauritania	Designated in 1999	2 October 2000	Not certified
Nigeria	Designated in 2000	2 October 2000	Not certified

*   This country expressed no interest in participating in the AGOA.

**   Sierra Leone has been designated as eligible, but an effective date of eligibility will be determined by the USTR in conjunction with other agencies.

***   These countries were not designated for ordinary GSP benefits until recently.

Figure 1
Share of US imports from AGOA countries enjoying preferences

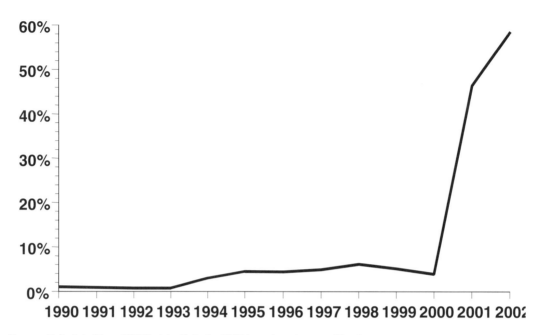

Source: Calculated from USITC data. Data for 2002 based on January–March.

The averages shown in figure 2 are likewise distorted by the overwhelming importance of low-tariff energy products in US imports from the region. Prior to AGOA, average US tariffs on imports from these countries hovered in the range of 0.8–1.6 per cent, which is at or below the average for US imports from all sources (see table 1). There was almost no difference between the average tariffs imposed on non-preferential imports and those imposed on all imports. With AGOA in place, the average tariff on all imports from the region has declined slightly.

The data in table 5 offer further details on the importance of oil and gas in US imports from the region, as well as the relative significance of apparel products. Both of these sectors merit special attention. Although oil and gas accounted for over half of all US imports from sub-Saharan African countries in 2001, they originated in just eight of the region's countries. Any observations on the tariff treatment of these products are therefore irrelevant to the other 40 countries. AGOA is much more significant for apparel products, because these items are exported by nearly all countries in the region and because they are subject to relatively high tariff and quota barriers. Paradoxically, the apparel products that account for a much smaller share of total US imports from the region may account for a larger share of real preferences than does the oil and gas sector. This is due to the much higher tariffs applied to apparel on an NTR basis, and hence the larger margins of preference.

Figure 2
Tariffs on US imports from AGOA countries

Average tariffs on US imports from 36 AGOA-designated countries

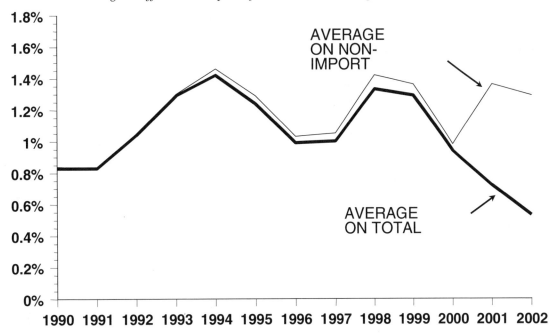

Source: Calculated from USICT data. Data for 2002 based on January–March.

Simple measures such as a programme's product coverage or average tariff rates are too crude to offer much guidance on the value of preferences. A more sophisticated standard of judgement will not just review the share of imports that enter duty-free, but will also take into account how the programme departs from the status quo and the magnitude of the margins of preference that it extends. This requires that we take into account the treatment that specific countries and products received prior to the advent of the programme. Many of the products that the US imports from these countries are already duty-free on an NTR basis, especially raw materials. Among the products that are dutiable, many are subject to relatively low duties; the aforementioned case of crude oil is a particularly significant example of this phenomenon. Moreover, nearly all of the beneficiaries of the AGOA had already received GSP treatment, and most of them were also eligible for the broader product coverage that is granted to LDCs. All of these points tend to militate against the conclusion that the AGOA benefits will be substantial.

Table 5
Composition of US imports from all sub-Saharan African countries, 2001

Actual dollars, customs value, imports for consumption

Country	Oil & gas	Apparel	Other	Total
Oil exporters	12,336,490,870	656,282	2,509,343,682	14,846,490,834
Nigeria	7,347,700,177	271,555	1,568,504,584	8,916,476,316
Angola	2,655,588,556	0	120,080,959	2,775,669,515
Gabon	1,485,385,588	0	246,285,529	1,731,671,117
Congo (ROC)	345,146,895	0	112,753,986	457,900,881
Equatorial Guinea	327,081,704	0	68,527,400	395,609,104
Congo (DROC)	108,302,262	2,517	39,408,692	147,713,471
Cameroon	44,011,710	252,691	57,362,750	101,627,151
Côte d'Ivoire	23,273,978	129,519	296,419,782	319,823,279
Apparel exporters	0	988,312,121	5,225,696,217	6,214,008,338
Mauritius	0	238,258,995	36,868,014	275,127,009
Lesotho	0	216,776,087	389,160	217,165,247
South Africa	0	183,485,733	4,246,053,453	4,429,539,186
Madagascar	0	178,702,492	93,088,801	271,791,293
Kenya	0	64,459,944	64,122,510	128,582,454
Swaziland	0	48,077,001	16,959,010	65,036,011
Zimbabwe	0	14,344,339	76,215,462	90,559,801
Malawi	0	12,384,697	59,415,637	71,800,334
Botswana	0	2,923,881	18,193,739	21,117,620
Sierra Leone	0	1,367,748	3,272,715	4,640,463
Cape Verde	0	1,201,257	294,692	1,495,949
Ethiopia	0	403,445	28,637,650	29,041,095
Ghana	0	245,528	185,145,760	185,391,288
Zambia	0	217,980	15,366,330	15,584,310
Mozambique	0	179,179	6,880,879	7,060,058
Central African Republic	0	126,412	2,237,262	2,363,674
Namibia	0	98,265	37,746,316	37,844,581
Somalia	0	68,726	274,569	343,295
United Rep. of Tanzania	0	61,545	27,167,662	27,229,207
Guinea	0	35,561	87,796,692	87,832,253
Níger	0	33,677	1,392,981	1,426,658
Seychelles	0	24,902	23,675,863	23,700,765
Senegal	0	28,603	102,315,901	102,344,504
Mali	0	28,201	6,177,175	6,205,376
Gambia	0	16,745	215,608	232,353
Uganda	0	12,975	17,822,377	17,835,352

Continued next page

Country	Oil & gas	Apparel	Other	Total
Burkina Faso	0	4,322	4,996,431	5,000,753
Togo	0	3,612	12,579,207	12,582,819
Sudan	0	1,690	3,383,699	3,385,389
Benin	0	1,580	1,284,756	1,286,336
Liberia	0	1,404	42,556,790	42,558,194
Mauritania	0	1,003	292,536	293,539
Eritrea	0	420	88,166	88,586
Burundi	0	360	2,788,414	2,788,774
All other	0	0	24,733,812	24,733,812
Comoros	0	0	10,568,080	10,568,080
Rwanda	0	0	7,220,871	7,220,871
Chad	0	0	5,653,051	5,653,051
Djibouti	0	0	950,571	950,571
Sao Tome & Principe	0	0	322,306	322,306
Guinea-Bissau	0	0	18,933	18,933
All sub-Saharan	12,336,490,870	964,234,591	8,724,008,302	21,060,499,172

Source: Calculated from USITC data.

An ideal analysis of AGOA's potential impact on countries' exports to the United States would be based upon near-perfect knowledge of the exporters' production, US barriers and the relationship between them. To simplify, we might distinguish here between four general categories of goods:

1. Those items that countries already produce and export to the United States. These are the easiest items to identify, as they can be found simply by reviewing US import data.
2. Those items that countries already produce and export, but do not ship in large quantities to the United States. These additional items could be identified by comparing a country's export data with US import data.
3. Those items that countries already produce but do not export at all. Identification of these products would require substantial information about current economic conditions in a country.
4. Those items that countries do not yet produce but which represent industries that could be developed through new investment. This is the most difficult category of goods to identify, especially if one wishes to track the plans of domestic and foreign investors.[22]

Unfortunately, sufficient data do not exist to conduct a dynamic analysis that takes into account all four product categories. For the purposes of this preliminary assessment we are confined to a static analysis that is limited to the items in the first category. A more ambitious research project might expand this analysis to take into account the second category, but it is doubtful that sufficient data

[22] For statistical and anecdotal evidence on new US investment in the region, see USTR, *2002 AGOA Report*, pp. 30–32.

could be assembled in most sub-Saharan African countries to conduct analyses that include the third and especially the fourth categories.

The basic method here is based on three simple steps. First, we identify the principal products that the United States imports from a beneficiary country. For the purposes of this analysis, these are defined as the top 25 products on an eight-digit HTS basis; for most sub-Saharan African countries that standard will capture at least 90 per cent of all products shipped to the United States. Second, we determine for the exporting country the tariff treatment that each of these products received (a) prior to AGOA and (b) under the country's new status. At the crudest level, this means identifying the duty-free coverage before and after designation. Third, we examine the margins of preference for any items that are newly eligible for preferential treatment.

Table 6 undertakes such an analysis for all 48 of the sub-Saharan African countries, summarizing the tariff treatment of the top 25 products that the United States imported from these countries in 2001. The data show that 15 of the 25 products, accounting for nearly one fifth of the value of these leading imports, were already duty-free on an NTR basis prior to AGOA. This means that neither the AGOA nor any other preferential programme could offer any margin of preference in access to the US market for these products. None of the top 25 products was eligible for duty-free treatment under the ordinary GSP, but six of them (over three fourths by value) were eligible for duty-free treatment under the GSP when imported from LDCs. The value of AGOA benefits here depends on a country's GSP status: coverage does not expand at all for LDCs, but goes from zero to 76.2 per cent for all other beneficiary countries. None of the top 25 products were eligible for duty-free treatment solely for AGOA beneficiaries. Three of the products representing 3.4 per cent of the value were in the textile and apparel category, and are thus eligible for duty- and quota-free treatment only when (a) they are imported from a country that has received certification for these benefits and (b) they meet the AGOA rules of origin. A special category consists of US goods returned, which generally means the value of US inputs included in items that are made in production-sharing operations. They are duty-free.

The data in table 6 can be assessed in two ways. The crudest form of analysis is to assess the overall expansion in duty-free coverage. If we were to treat this region as one large but ordinary GSP beneficiary (i.e. not an LDC), 20.3 per cent of the value of its top 25 products already received duty-free treatment pre-AGOA (i.e.19.0 per cent on an NTR basis, none under GSP and 1.3 per cent as "special"). That figure rises to 96.5 per cent if the country is designated for partial AGOA benefits (i.e. all of the items that had been eligible for duty-free treatment for LDC GSP countries are now treated preferentially). Assuming that the country is also certified for textile and apparel benefits and can meet the rules of origin requirements for these items, the duty-free coverage rises to 100 per cent.[23] In other words, for an ordinary GSP country that receives full AGOA benefits the coverage of preferential treatment rises by 79.7 percentage points. On the face of it, that would appear to be a very significant increase. The rise would not be nearly as great for an LDC, insofar as most of those imports were already GSP-eligible before AGOA. For such a country, the only potential for increased duty-free treatment comes in the textile and apparel sector.

---

[23] Note that these numbers do not necessarily add up to 100 per cent owing to rounding errors.

Table 6
Top 25 US imports from all sub-Saharan African countries, 2001

Millions of dollars, customs value, imports for consumption

HTS item and description	Imports	NTR tariff
Duty-free on NTR Basis (19.0% of top 25 products)	**3,394**	
7110.11.00 Platinum, unwrought or in powder form	802	Free
7110.21.00 Palladium, unwrought or in powder form	404	Free
7102.31.00 Non-industrial diamonds, unworked	340	Free
1801.00.00 Cocoa beans, whole or broken, raw or roasted	247	Free
2713.11.00 Coke, petroleum, not calcined	225	Free
7110.31.00 Rhodium, unwrought or in powder form	218	Free
2711.29.00 Petroleum gases and other gaseous hydrocarbons	183	Free
2711.11.00 Natural gas, liquefied	176	Free
7102.39.00 Non-industrial diamonds, worked, not mounted or set	170	Free
8421.39.40 Catalytic converters	166	Free
2620.90.50 Slag over 40% titanium*	140	Free
0905.00.00 Vanilla beans	90	Free
2711.12.00 Propane, liquefied	88	Free
2901.29.50 Unsaturated acyclic hydrocarbons	77	Free
2606.00.00 Aluminium ores and concentrates	68	Free
Duty-free for all GSP countries (0% of top 25 products)	**0**	
Duty-free for LDC GSP countries (76.2% of top 25 products)	**13,599**	
2709.00.20 Petroleum oils and oils from bituminous minerals	11,730	10.5¢/bbl.
2710.00.05 Distillate and residual fuel oils from bitum. mins.*	852	5.25¢/bbl.
2710.00.10 Distillate and residual fuel oils from bitum. mins.*	597	10.5¢/bbl.
8703.24.00 Motor cars & vehicles	256	2.5%
2710.00.25 Naphthas from petro. oils*	85	10.5¢/bbl.
2710.00.45 Mixtures of hydrocarbons*	79	10.5¢/bbl.
Duty-free only for AGOA countries (0% of top 25 products)	**0**	
Textile & apparel (3.4% of top 25 products)		
6110.20.20 Sweaters etc. of cotton	214	17.3%
6203.42.40 Men's or boys' trousers and shorts	202	16.8%
6204.62.40 Women's or girls' trousers etc. of cotton	196	16.8%
Special (1.3% of top 25 products)		
9801.00.10 US goods returned	238	
Subtotal (top 25 products account for 84.7% of total)	17,843	
All other	3,217	
Total	21,060	

* Product for which the 2002 version of the HTS uses a somewhat different classification than was used in 2001.

It having been established which products might be transferred from dutiable to duty-free treatment, the next step is to consider the margins of preference for these items. Let us once again assume that the data in table 6 apply to imports from an ordinary GSP country. Six items are newly eligible for duty-free treatment when that country receives partial AGOA benefits. Five of these items are in the petroleum sector, and — as already reviewed above — tariffs in this sector are quite low. The 10.5¢ per tariff on HTS item 2709.00.20, for example, translates into a 0.42 per cent *ad valorem* tariff when oil is valued at $25 per barrel. The other energy products are also subject to relatively low tariffs. The only non-oil item in this category is certain motor cars; these are subject to a tariff of 2.5 per cent. That rate is slightly above the average US rate, but still confers a relatively low margin of preference. In general, one can conclude that while these six products account for a large share of US imports from the beneficiary countries, their new duty-free status extends small margins of preference.

Things are quite different for the three textile and apparel products shown in table 6. Here the tariff rates range between 16.8 and 17.3 per cent ad valorem, which are quite high by US standards. Moreover, these items are at least hypothetically subject to quotas until 2005 when imported from countries that do not have FTAs with the United States or receive preferential treatment under the AGOA or CBI programs. We can therefore conclude that the AGOA benefits for these three products are substantial, provided that the exporting country is certified for the benefits and meets the programme's rules of origin.

These observations suggest that the most important AGOA benefits are indeed in the textile and apparel sector. Most of the other preferences were already in place for LDCs. Moreover, they tend to be in product sectors that would otherwise be subject to relatively low tariffs and therefore confer relatively low margins of preference.

The data presented in table 6 are region-wide, and the experience of individual countries under the AGOA might vary considerably. This same exercise is therefore repeated for all 48 sub-Saharan African countries in the Appendix 1. For each sub-Saharan country the analysis shows the top 25 US imports in 2001 (or all imports if there were fewer than 25 items in United States imports from the country), broken down according to the tariff status of the products. For example, table A-1 summarizes US imports from Angola. The overall pattern for this country is similar to what was shown in table 6 for sub-Saharan Africa as a whole, with petroleum products predominating. As an LDC, Angola already receives duty-free treatment for these items under the GSP. It has not yet been designated for AGOA benefits, but the data in Table A-1 suggest that such designation would have no consequences for the principal US imports from Angola. By contrast, the data for Benin in table A-2 indicate that at least four products exported by that country could benefit if Benin is certified for the textile and apparel provisions of AGOA.

Such country-by-country examinations can produce a mass of observations that it is difficult to decipher. Table 7 helps to make sense of this mass by summarizing the overall results for countries, grouped according to the categories already used in table 4. It must be stressed that this summary is based solely on the product coverage of the programme with respect to countries and groups of countries; it is still necessary to refer to the individual tables in the Appendix in order to examine the tariff rates (and hence the margins of preference) for specific products. The summary nevertheless brings out some useful points. First, the AGOA's only significant benefits for LDCs are in the textile and apparel provisions. As was already pointed out, there is only one LDC exporting only one non-textile product that was not previously eligible for duty-free treatment. About half of the LDCs in the

Table 7
Tariff treatment of principal US imports from sub-Saharan Africa, 2001

Lightly shaded areas show preferences that are newly granted through countries' status under AGOA;
Darkly shaded areas show preferences that could be granted to countries under AGOA

	NTR Duty-free	GSP	LDC-GSP	AGOA only	Textiles & apparel	Special
LDCs not designated for AGOA benefits						
Angola	0.2	0.0	99.6	0.0	0.0	0.2
Burundi	91.8	0.0	0.0	0.0	0.0	8.2
Burkina Faso	3.2	2.0	0.0	0.0	0.1	94.6
Comoros	99.7	0.0	0.0	0.0	0.0	0.3
Dem. Rep. of the Congo	19.5	6.7	73.7	0.0	0.0	0.1
Equatorial Guinea	10.7	6.3	82.2	0.0	0.0	0.8
Gambia	49.2	9.6	12.1	0.0	27.9	1.2
Somalia	62.2	0.0	17.6	0.0	20.1	0.1
Togo	45.1	1.4	30.4	0.0	4.1	19.0
Simple average	42.4	2.9	35.1	0.0	5.8	13.8
Incremental gain in duty-free access — (1) thus far: 0.0%; (2) potentially: 5.8%.						
LDCs with partial AGOA benefits						
Benin	63.3	14.2	0.0	0.0	2.5	20.0
Cape Verde	1.9	5.8	11.8	0.0	80.3	0.2
Central African Rep.	88.1	3.9	0.0	0.0	5.3	2.7
Chad	98.7	0.8	0.0	0.0	0.0	0.5
Republic of the Congo	6.8	0.3	92.8	0.0	0.0	0.2
Djibouti	12.9	4.7	0.0	0.0	0.0	82.4
Guinea	98.3	0.6	0.0	0.0	0.0	1.1
Guinea-Bissau	100.0	0.0	0.0	0.0	0.0	0.0
Mali	52.4	6.3	0.0	0.0	0.8	40.5
Niger	28.0	34.1	9.7	0.0	3.5	25.0
Rwanda	94.1	1.9	3.7	0.0	0.0	0.3
Sao Tome & Principe	68.1	21.3	0.0	0.0	5.9	4.7
Sierra Leone	30.4	19.4	0.0	0.0	50.3	0.0
Simple average	57.2	8.7	9.1	0.0	11.4	13.7
Incremental gain in duty-free access — (1) thus far: 0.0%; (2) potentially: 11.4%.						
LDCs with full AGOA benefits						
Ethiopia	94.2	0.9	0.8	0.0	2.0	2.0
Lesotho	0.0	0.0	0.0	0.0	100.0	0.0
Madagascar	32.6	0.9	0.0	0.0	66.4	0.0
Malawi	18.8	11.2	52.8	0.0	17.1	0.05
Mozambique	20.4	74.8	0.0	0.0	2.5	2.3
United Rep. of Tanzania	88.8	1.4	3.0	0.0	1.4	5.4
Uganda	97.1	1.7	0.0	0.0	0.1	1.2
Zambia	87.0	7.2	0.2	1.1	1.4	3.1
Simple average	54.9	12.3	7.1	0.1	23.9	1.8
Incremental gain in duty-free access — 24.0%.						

Continued next page

	NTR Duty-free	GSP	LDC-GSP	AGOA only	Textiles & apparel	Special
GSP beneficiaries not designated for AGOA benefits						
Zimbabwe	12.8	52.4	17.5	0.0	17.3	0.0
Incremental gain in duty-free access — (1) thus far: 0.0%; (2) potentially: 34.8%.						
GSP beneficiaries with partial AGOA benefits						
Côte d'Ivoire	74.0	4.2	21.4	0.0	0.0	0.4
Seychelles	69.7	18.7	0.0	0.0	0.0	11.5
Simple average	71.9	11.5	10.7	0.0	0.0	6.0
Incremental gain in duty-free access — (1) thus far: 10.7%; (2) potentially: 0.0%.						
GSP beneficiaries with full AGOA benefits						
Botswana	74.5	8.6	0.0	0.0	13.8	3.1
Cameroon	13.4	0.5	83.1	0.0	1.8	1.2
Ghana	61.6	4.3	31.4	0.0	0.0	2.6
Kenya	36.2	1.7	4.0	0.0	53.7	4.4
Mauritius	5.1	5.1	0.0	0.0	88.4	1.4
Namibia	95.4	0.2	0.0	0.0	0.3	4.2
Senegal	2.9	1.1	5.4	0.0	1.3	89.4
South Africa	78.3	5.9	9.7	0.0	2.7	3.4
Swaziland	14.2	10.0	0.3	0.0	74.9	0.3
Simple average	42.4	4.2	14.9	0.0	26.3	12.2
Incremental gain in duty-free access — 41.2%.						
Non-GSP beneficiaries not designated for AGOA benefits						
Liberia	98.2	0.1	0.1	0.0	0.1	1.5
Sudan	98.8	0.1	0.0	0.0	0.0	1.2
Simple average	98.5	0.1	0.1	0.0	0.1	1.4
Incremental gain in duty-free access — potentially: 0.3%.						
Non-GSP beneficiaries with partial AGOA benefits						
Eritrea	60.0	42.6	0.0	0.0	0.5	0.0
Gabon	6.0	0.0	94.0	0.0	0.0	0.1
Mauritania	54.4	0.0	12.8	0.0	0.3	32.5
Nigeria	10.9	0.0	89.1	0.0	0.0	0.0
Simple average	32.8	10.7	49.0	0.0	0.2	8.2
Incremental gain in duty-free access — (1) thus far: 59.7%: (2) potentially: 0.2%.						

Note: The "share eligible for duty-free treatment before AGOA" consists of the percentage of imports from the country in 2001 that could have qualified for duty-free treatment on either an NTR or a preferential basis, assuming full use of all preferential programmes for which the country was eligible. The "share eligible for duty-free treatment under AGOA" additionally includes all products that are newly eligible for duty-free treatment under the country's current status. In both cases, all "special" imports are assumed to enter duty-free.

Source: Calculated from the data in tables A-1 through A-48 (appendix).

region export little or no textile and apparel products to the United States, but for several countries this sector is very significant; in four cases it accounts for over half of all US imports from a country. The table nevertheless shows that only eight of the LDCs have been certified for textile and apparel benefits thus far. Unless the other 22 countries achieve the same status — and in nine cases they have not yet been granted even partial AGOA benefits — the programme is not likely to make a significant difference in their exports to the United States.

The programme may be much more beneficial for the non-LDC countries in the region, some of which were not even designated for the ordinary GSP until recently. The potential here varies greatly from one country to another. Liberia, Namibia and Sudan all depend heavily on exports of raw materials that are already eligible for duty-free treatment on an NTR basis; this means that neither the GSP nor AGOA can have an impact on their principal products. (The programme could nevertheless help to stimulate shipments of non-traditional products.) At the other extreme are countries such as Cameroon, Gabon and Nigeria that had previously been subject to duties on most of their exports to the United States; they now enjoy virtually complete duty-free access to the US market. However, closer look at their export profiles shows that these three countries' new benefits are primarily in the area of petroleum products,[24] the low tariffs on which diminish the real value of the apparent gain in preferential access.

Most of the non-LDC countries in the region that show relatively large gains in duty-free coverage depend heavily on exports of either oil and gas or on textiles and apparel. Once again, therefore, the most significant benefits of the programme are likely to flow to those countries that obtain certification for these additional benefits and manage to meet the AGOA rules of origin requirements.

The AGOA rules of origin for textile and apparel products were the subject of lengthy bargaining in the United States Congress. These internal negotiations were the principal reason why it took three years for the Clinton administration to win approval for the programme in Congress. The rules are quite strict, as they generally require that apparel articles must be made "from fabrics wholly formed and cut in the United States, from yarns wholly formed in the United States". There are nevertheless exceptions to this general rule. Preferential treatment can be extended to products made with yarns or fibers that are not available either in the United States or Africa, or to apparel made from cashmere or silk yarns. The bill limits duty-free access to the US market for African apparel made with African fabric or yarn, subject to a cap of 1.5 to 3.5 per cent of overall US global apparel imports over eight years. A special provision will allow countries with an annual per capita income below $1,500 to use third-country fabric in African-made apparel for four years.

The data in table 8 indicate why the legislative allies of the US textile and apparel industry fought so long and so hard to obtain such strict rules. For nearly 20 years US policy has tacitly sought to use preferential trade agreements and programmes as a means of extending the life of a dying industry. Finished apparel products can be imported from certain partners on preferential bases, but only if they incorporate the requisite amount of US goods and/or labour. If the United States is going to import shirts and skirts, according to the logic of this policy they should at least be made from

---

[24] See tables A-6, A-18 and A-34.

Table 8

Ratio of US imports to exports in the textile and apparel sector with selected trading partners, 2001

Thousands of current dollars; imports are for consumption, customs value; exports are domestic, FAS value

	US imports			US exports			Ratio of total
	Fabrics	Apparel	Total	Fabrics	Apparel	Total	Imports: Exports
Duty- and quota-free treatment							
Canada	1,084,416	1,754,289	2,838,705	1,244,067	494,556	1,738,623	1.63:1
México	478,241	8,111,553	8,589,794	2,675,626	1,906,882	4,582,508	1.87:1
Caribbean Basin Initiative	17,600	9,603,233	9,620,833	1,532,832	3,072,172	4,605,004	2.08:1
African Growth & Opportunity Act	14,010	949,791	963,801	34,343	5,740	40,083	24.05:1
Dutiable, quota-free treatment							
Andean Trade Preferences Act	17,152	761,840	796,144	68,232	43,498	111,730	7.13:1
Dutiable and subject to quota							
China	1,853,811	8,597,110	10,450,921	74,200	30,076	104,276	100.22:1
Taiwan, Province of China	419,783	1,839,555	2,259,338	28,395	12,510	40,905	55.23:1
Hong Kong (China)	163,131	4,278,148	4,441,279	185,922	36,344	222,266	19.98:1
Rep. of Korea	615,271	2,281,055	2,896,326	49,237	31,679	80,916	35.79:1
Pakistan	329,155	1,020,053	1,349,208	3,102	125	3,227	418.10:1
India	202,335	1,941,256	2,143,591	11,071	710	11,781	181.95:1

Source: Calculated from USITC data.

US fabric. The Caribbean Basin Initiative was the first step in this policy, having been expanded in 1986 to provide preferential quota treatment (but not tariff exemptions) to qualifying imports from the region. NAFTA works on the same principle, but sets even stricter rules of origin. When Congress approved the extension of duty-free treatment to Caribbean Basin textile and apparel products in 2000, it insisted that these new benefits be conditioned on the stricter NAFTA rules of origin. The expanded CBI benefits, and stricter rules, were part of the Trade and Development Act of 2000. This was the bill that enacted AGOA into law. The AGOA rules of origin for textile and apparel products are thus merely the latest manifestation of a well-established policy.

The only difference between AGOA and its predecessors is that this programme has not been in place long enough to bring about significant changes in the pattern of US textile and apparel trade with the beneficiary countries. The data in table 8 show that these patterns are quite different for preferential and non-preferential imports. While the United States still has a deficit in this sector with Canada, Mexico and the CBI countries, its exports to these countries counterbalance a large share of the imports. Indeed, many of those exports *are* the imports: the United States exports fabric, semi-finished products and the like to offshore plants in Mexico and the Caribbean Basin, where they are made into finished products and re-exported to the United States. There is little or no such production-sharing between the United States and the Asian countries; imports from these countries greatly outweigh US exports. The chief goal of the AGOA rules of origin is to encourage a pattern of trade with African countries that more closely resembles the NAFTA and CBI pattern, in which the finished products that are imported on a preferential basis incorporate significant amounts of US content. The data in table 8 suggest that this objective has not yet been reached, but it can be anticipated that the pattern will evolve further in the years to come.

Appendix

**Tariff treatment of the top US imports of products
from sub-Saharan African countries in 2001**

Table A-1. Top 25 US imports from Angola, 2001

Actual dollars, customs value, imports for consumption

HTS Item and Description	Imports	NTR Tariff
Duty-Free on NTR Basis (0.2% of top 25 products)	**5,912,694**	
2711.29.00 Petroleum gases and other gaseous hydrocarbons	2,339,716	Free
2711.19.00 Liquefied petroleum gases and gaseous hydrocarbons	1,080,372	Free
2711.13.00 Butanes, liquefied	1,018,172	Free
2713.11.00 Coke, petroleum, not calcined	659,429	Free
9705.00.00 Collections and collectors' pieces of zoological etc. interest	242,797	Free
2503.00.00 Sulfur of all kinds, other than sublimed etc., sulfur	151,841	Free
2711.14.00 Ethylene etc., liquefied	98,087	Free
7116.20.50 Precious stone articles	86,637	Free
2711.12.00 Propane, liquefied	76,464	Free
8471.90.00 Magnetic or optical readers machines	57,960	Free
8431.39.00 Parts for use with lifting etc. machinery	50,000	Free
9030.40.00 Instruments for telecommunications	20,795	Free
8413.11.00 Pumps of the type used in filling-stations	12,726	Free
8525.20.90 Transmission apparatus	12,698	Free
8471.41.00 Digital computer machines, nonportable or over 10 kg	5,000	Free
Duty-Free For All GSP Countries (0.01% of top 25 products)	**368,654**	
8537.10.90 Boards etc., with apparatus for electric control	240,000	2.7%
9006.91.00 Parts for photographic cameras, not cinematographic	120,000	5.8%
8481.80.30 Taps, cocks, valves & similar appliances of iron or steel	8,654	5.6%
Duty-Free For LDC GSP Countries (99.6% of top 25 products)	**2,763,492,038**	
2709.00.20 Petroleum oils and oils from bituminous minerals	2,643,725,636	10.5¢/bbl.
2710.00.05 Distillate and residual fuel oils from bitum. mins.*	85,719,709	5.25¢/bbl.
2710.00.25 Naphthas from petro oils*	18,755,335	10.5¢/bbl.
2710.00.10 Distillate and residual fuel oils from bitum. mins.*	7,932,475	10.5¢/bbl.
2709.00.10 Petroleum oils and oils from bitum. mins.	7,348,196	5.25¢/bbl.
2710.00.15 Motor fuel from petro oils and bitum. mins.*	10,687	52.5¢/bbl.
Duty-Free Only For AGOA Countries (0% of top 25 products)	**0**	
Textile & Apparel (0% of top 25 products)	**0**	
Special (0.2% of top 25 products)		
9801.00.10 US goods returned	5,864,773	
Subtotal (Top 25 Products Account for 99.9 % of Total)	2,775,638,159	
All Other	31,356	
Total	2,775,669,515	

* : Product for which the 2002 version of the HTS uses a somewhat different classification than was used in 2001.

Table A-2. Top 12 US imports from Benin, 2001

Actual dollars, customs value, imports for consumption

HTS Item and Description	Imports	NTR Tariff
Duty-Free on NTR Basis (63.3% of top 12 products)	**813,973**	
0106.00.50 Live animals other than horses, asses, mules etc.*	698,417	Free
4407.29.00 Tropical wood sawn etc., over 6 mm thick	87,856	Free
9706.00.00 Antiques of an age exceeding one hundred years	23,000	Free
1106.20.00 Flour, meal and powder of sago, or of roots etc.*	4,700	Free
Duty-Free For All GSP Countries (14.2% of top 12 products)	**182,287**	
4420.10.00 Wooden statuettes and other wood ornaments	178,319	3.2%
1209.91.80 Vegetable seeds of a kind used for sowing	3,968	1.5¢/kg.
Duty-Free For LDC GSP Countries (0% of top 12 products)	**0**	
Duty-Free Only For AGOA Countries (0% of top 12 products)	**0**	
Textile & Apparel (2.5% of top 12 products)	**32,541**	
5208.52.30 Printed plain weave fabrics of cotton	17,208	6.7%
5208.32.30 Dyed plain weave fabrics of cotton	13,183	7.5%
6204.42.30 Women's or girls' dresses, etc. of cotton	1,580	9.2%
6002.92.10 Circular knit fabric wholly of cotton etc.*	570	9.0%
Special (20.0% of top 12 products)	**257,535**	
9801.00.10 US goods returned	256,522	
9999.95.00 Informal entries under $1251	1,013	
Subtotal (Top 12 Products Account for 100% of Total)	1,286,336	1,286,336
All Other	0	0
Total	1,286,336	1,286,336

* : Product for which the 2002 version of the HTS uses a somewhat different classification than was used in 2001.

Table A-3. Top 25 United States Imports from Botswana, 2001

Actual dollars, customs value, imports for consumption

HTS Item and Description	Imports	NTR Tariff
Duty-Free on NTR Basis (74.5% of top 25 products)	**15,687,968**	
7102.31.00 Nonindustrial diamonds, unworked	11,539,967	Free
7102.29.00 Industrial diamonds, worked, but not mounted or set	2,791,127	Free
7102.39.00 Nonindustrial diamonds, worked, but not mounted or set	613,895	Free
7102.10.00 Diamonds, unsorted, whether or not worked	444,307	Free
7102.21.30 Industrial diamonds (other than miners' diamonds)	186,033	Free
0302.39.00 Tunas except fillets, livers, roes, etc.	67,062	Free
8414.80.05 Turbocharger and supercharger air compressors	20,666	Free
9705.00.00 Collections and collectors' pieces of zoological etc.	13,910	Free
0302.32.00 Yellowfin tunas	11,001	Free
Duty-Free For All GSP Countries (8.6% of top 25 products)	**1,807,902**	
7113.19.21 Gold rope necklaces and neck chains	986,012	5.0%
7113.19.50 Precious metal (other than silver) articles of jewelry	379,368	5.5%
7113.19.29 Gold necklaces and neck chains (other than of rope)	361,116	5.5%
8504.40.95 Static converters (for example, rectifiers)	42,120	1.5%
4302.19.60 Tanned/dressed whole furskins, not assembled, not dyed	20,018	3.5%
0106.00.10 Live birds, other than poultry*	19,268	1.8%
Duty-Free For LDC GSP Countries (0% of top 25 products)	**0**	
Duty-Free Only For AGOA Countries (0% of top 25 products)	**0**	
Textile & Apparel (13.8% of top 25 products)	**2,902,473**	
6203.42.40 Men's or boys' trousers and shorts of cotton	1,395,519	16.8%
6104.62.20 Women's or girls' trousers etc. of cotton	399,777	15.3%
6110.30.30 Sweaters etc. of manmade fibers	476,675	32.4%
6201.93.30 Men's or boys' anoraks, etc. of manmade fibers	195,043	7.2%
6109.10.00 T-shirts, singlets, etc. of cotton	190,746	17.4%
6102.20.00 Women's or girls' overcoats etc. of cotton	89,724	16.1%
6104.63.20 Women's or girls' trousers etc. of synthetic fibers	81,118	28.6%
6204.62.40 Women's or girls' trousers etc. of cotton	73,871	16.8%
Special (3.1% of top 25 products)	**649,382**	
9801.00.10 US goods returned	579,504	
9999.95.00 Informal entries under $1251	69,878	
Subtotal (Top 25 Products Account for 99.7% of Total)	21,047,725	
All Other	69,895	
Total	21,117,620	

* : Product for which the 2002 version of the HTS uses a somewhat different classification than was used in 2001.

Table A-4. Top 25 United States Imports from Burkina Faso, 2001

Actual dollars, customs value, imports for consumption

HTS Item and Description		Imports	NTR Tariff
Duty-Free on NTR Basis (3.2% of top 25 products)		**160,778**	
9706.00.00	Antiques of an age exceeding one hundred years	52,150	Free
2401.10.53	Tobacco, not stemmed/stripped	32,614	Free
1602.50.10	Corned beef in airtight containers	31,418	Free
9705.00.00	Collections and collectors' pieces of zoological etc.	18,401	Free
1211.90.80	Plants and parts of plants used in perfumery, pharmacy etc.*	7,364	Free
6815.99.40	Articles of stone or of other mineral substances	5,700	Free
8306.29.00	Base metal statuettes and other ornaments	4,057	Free
4602.10.07	Baskets and bags of bamboo wickerwork	3,237	Free
6913.10.50	Porcelain or china (other than bone china) statuettes etc.	3,000	Free
8473.30.10	Parts & Accessories of computers, printed circuit assembles	2,837	Free
Duty-Free For All GSP Countries (2.0% of top 25 products)		**101,657**	
4420.10.00	Wooden statuettes and other wood ornaments	25,433	3.2%
9206.00.80	Percussion musical instruments (other than drums, etc.)	25,335	5.3%
9206.00.20	Percussion musical instruments; drums	24,359	4.8%
4602.10.18	Baskets and bags of vegetable material	12,449	4.5%
0804.50.80	Guavas, mangoes, and mangosteens, dried	7,814	1.5¢/kg.
3920.42.50	Nonadhesive plates etc. of polymers of vinyl chloride*	2,556	5.8%
3906.90.50	Acrylic polymers (except plastics or elastomers)	2,027	4.2%
5209.51.30	Printed plain weave certified hand-loomed fabrics of cotton	1,684	3.6%
Duty-Free For LDC GSP Countries (0% of top 25 products)		**0**	
Duty-Free Only For AGOA Countries (0% of top 25 products)		**0**	
Textile & Apparel (0.1% of top 25 products)		**5,060**	
6304.92.00	Furnishing articles of cotton	1,800	6.5%
6117.10.60	Shawls, scarves, mufflers, mantillas, veils, etc.	1,060	9.6%
6204.13.20	Women's or girls' suits of synthetic fibers	850	[Complex]
6204.42.30	Women's or girls' dresses of cotton	800	9.2%
6211.42.00	Women's or girls' track suits etc. of cotton	550	8.2%
Special (94.6% of top 25 products)		**4,730,743**	
9801.00.10	US goods returned	4,550,000	
9999.95.00	Informal entries under $1251	180,743	
Subtotal (Top 25 Products Account for 99.9% of Total)		4,998,238	
All Other		2,515	
Total		5,000,753	

* : Product for which the 2002 version of the HTS uses a somewhat different classification than was used in 2001.

Table A-5. Top 8 United States Imports from Burundi, 2001

Actual dollars, customs value, imports for consumption

HTS Item and Description	Imports	NTR Tariff
Duty-Free on NTR Basis (91.8 % of top 8 products)	**2,559,879**	
0901.11.00 Coffee, not roasted, not decaffeinated	2,395,257	Free
0301.10.00 Live ornamental fish	59,174	Free
9018.19.95 Electro-diagnostic apparatus	57,289	Free
9601.10.00 Ivory, worked and articles	45,790	Free
4907.00.00 Unused stamps of current/new issue in country	2,369	Free
Duty-Free For All GSP Countries (0% of top 8 products)	**0**	
Duty-Free For LDC GSP Countries (0% of top 8 products)	**0**	
Duty-Free Only For AGOA Countries (0% of top 8 products)	**0**	
Textile & Apparel (0.01% of top 8 products)	**360**	
6105.10.00 Men's or boys' shirts of cotton	360	20.0%
Special (8.2% of top 8 products)	**228,535**	
9801.00.10 US goods returned	217,840	
9999.95.00 Informal entries under $1251	10,695	
Subtotal (Top 8 Products Account for 100% of Total)	2,788,774	
All Other	0	
Total	2,788,774	

Table A-6. Top 25 US imports from Cameroon, 2001

Actual dollars, customs value, imports for consumption

HTS Item and Description	Imports	NTR Tariff
Duty-Free on NTR Basis (13.4% of top 25 products)	**13,401,505**	
4407.24.00 Virola, Mahogany, Imbuia and Balsa wood*	2,527,417	Free
4407.99.00 Nonconiferous woods sawn etc., over 6 mm thick	2,230,447	Free
4001.22.00 Technically specified natural rubber (TSNR)	1,788,982	Free
4407.29.00 Tropical wood sawn etc., over 6 mm thick	1,521,382	Free
0901.11.00 Coffee, not roasted, not decaffeinated	1,243,724	Free
2401.10.21 Wrapper tobacco, not stemmed/stripped	1,032,244	Free
1803.10.00 Cocoa paste, not defatted	918,554	Free
4408.39.00 Tropical wood, not over 6 mm thick	879,551	Free
4408.90.00 Nontropical, nonconiferous veneer sheets etc.	351,356	Free
4001.29.00 Natural rubber in primary forms other than latex etc.	250,891	Free
9706.00.00 Antiques of an age exceeding one hundred years	138,726	Free
9019.10.20 Mechano-therapy appliances and massage apparatus	127,160	Free
2401.10.53 Tobacco, not stemmed or stripped	116,906	Free
4406.10.00 Railway/tramway sleepers of wood, not impregnated	100,024	Free
9705.00.00 Collections and collectors' pieces of zoological etc.	88,489	Free
9403.60.80 Furniture of wooden	85,652	Free
Duty-Free For All GSP Countries (0.5% of top 25 products)	**521,657**	
4420.10.00 Wooden statuettes and other wood ornaments	149,107	3.2%
1803.20.00 Cocoa paste, wholly or partly defatted	272,167	0.2¢/kg.
1805.00.00 Cocoa powder, not containing added sugar etc.	100,383	0.52¢/kg.
Duty-Free For LDC GSP Countries (83.1% of top 25 products)	**83,031,232**	
2709.00.20 Petroleum oils and oils from bituminous minerals	44,011,710	10.5¢/bbl.
2710.00.05 Distillate and residual fuel oils from bitum. mins.*	39,019,522	5.25¢/bbl
Duty-Free Only For AGOA Countries (0% of top 25 products)	**0**	
Textile & Apparel (1.8% of top 25 products)	**1,770,358**	
5208.52.40 Printed plain weave fabrics of cotton of number 43-68	1,546,303	11.4%
6110.90.10 Sweaters, pullovers etc. of textile materials	224,055	1.9%
Special (1.2% of top 25 products)	**1,240,211**	
9801.00.10 US goods returned	1,097,774	
9999.95.00 Informal entries under $1251	142,437	
Subtotal (Top 25 Products Account for 98.4% of Total)	99,964,963	
All Other	1,662,188	
Total	101,627,151	

* : Product for which the 2002 version of the HTS uses a somewhat different classification than was used in 2001.

Table A-7. Top 22 US imports from Cape Verde, 2001

Actual dollars, customs value, imports for consumption

HTS Item and Description	Imports	NTR Tariff
Duty-Free on NTR Basis (1.9% of top 22 products)	**28,414**	
8471.90.00 Magnetic or optical readers	23,450	Free
2208.70.00 Liqueurs and cordials	2,482	Free
2208.90.30 Brandy in not over 4 liters, valued over $3.43/liter	2,482	Free
Duty-Free For All GSP Countries (5.8% of top 22 products)	**87,066**	
2202.90.90 Nonalcoholic beverages, not including fruit/vegetable juices	40,380	0.2¢/liter
1604.15.00 Prepared/preserved mackerel	14,140	3%
1604.19.30 Prepared/preserved fish in airtight containers	14,000	4%
7801.91.00 Lead (other than refined lead), unwrought	11,000	[Complex]
9010.90.90 Parts & Accessories for photographic labs	4,546	2.9%
9031.80.80 Measuring and checking instruments	3,000	1.7%
Duty-Free For LDC GSP Countries (11.8% of top 22 products)	**175,924**	
1604.14.10 Tunas and skipjack in airtight containers	123,620	35%
2208.40.40 Rum and tafia, in not over 4 liters, valued over $3/proof liter	52,304	4.3¢/pf.liter
Duty-Free Only For AGOA Countries (0% of top 22 products)	**0**	
Textile & Apparel (80.3% of top 22 products)	**1,201,257**	
6204.23.00 Women's or girls' ensembles of synthetic fibers	306,997	[Complex]
6204.44.40 Women's or girls' dresses of artificial fibers	169,652	16.2%
6206.90.00 Women's or girls' blouses, etc. of textile materials	146,412	6.8%
6211.43.00 Women's or girls' track suits, etc. of man-made fibers	143,717	16.2%
6204.33.50 Women's or girls' suit-type jackets, etc. of synthetic fibers	135,024	27.6%
6206.40.30 Women's or girls' blouses, etc. of manmade fibers	102,551	27.2%
6204.53.30 Women's or girls' skirts, etc. of synthetic fibers	94,428	16.2%
6204.63.35 Women's or girls' trousers, etc. of synthetic fibers	60,039	29.0%
6204.43.40 Women's or girls' dresses of synthetic fibers	41,717	16.2%
6205.30.20 Men's or boys' shirts of manmade fibers	720	[Complex]
Special (0.2% of top 22 products)	**3,288**	
9801.00.10 US goods returned	3,288	
Subtotal (Top 22 Products Account for 100% of Total)	1,495,949	
All Other	0	
Total	1,495,949	

Table A-8. Top 22 US imports from Central African Republic, 2001

Actual dollars, customs value, imports for consumption

HTS Item and Description	Imports	NTR Tariff
Duty-Free on NTR Basis (88.1% of top 22 products)	**2,082,329**	
7102.31.00 Nonindustrial diamonds, unworked	1,362,426	Free
2401.10.21 Wrapper tobacco, not stemmed/stripped	447,760	Free
1521.10.00 Vegetable waxes (other than triglycerides)	126,535	Free
6506.10.30 Safety headgear of reinforced or laminated plastics	58,584	Free
9026.90.60 Parts & Accessories for nonelectrical instruments	35,426	Free
4408.90.00 Nontropical, nonconiferous veneer sheets etc.	33,989	Free
7102.39.00 Nonindustrial diamonds, worked, but not mounted	7,695	Free
0302.69.20 Smelts, cusk, hake, etc.	6,741	Free
0902.30.00 Black tea (fermented) and partly fermented tea	2,173	Free
4103.90.00 Raw hides and skins of animals*	1,000	Free
Duty-Free For All GSP Countries (3.9% of top 22 products)	**91,041**	
7323.93.00 Stainless steel, table, kitchen etc.	43,465	2.0%
8503.00.95 Parts for use with the electronic motors, generating sets	21,301	3.0%
8708.99.67 Parts of motor vehicles; other parts of power trains	15,000	2.5%
8414.59.60 Fans	4,920	2.3%
6306.31.00 Sails for boats etc. of synthetic fibers	3,468	0.8%
9004.90.00 Spectacles, goggles etc. (other than sunglasses)	2,887	2.5%
Duty-Free For LDC GSP Countries (0% of top 22 products)	**0**	
Duty-Free Only For AGOA Countries (0% of top 22 products)	**0**	
Textile & Apparel (5.3% of top 22 products)	**126,412**	
6108.22.90 Women's or girls' briefs etc. of man-made fibers	110,172	15.8%
6108.21.00 Women's or girls' briefs etc. of cotton	15,537	7.7%
6212.90.00 Braces, suspenders, garters ets.	703	6.7%
Special (2.7% of top 22 products)	**63,892**	
9999.95.00 Informal entries under $1251	43,487	
9801.00.10 US goods returned	16,647	
9801.00.25 Articles reimported	3,758	
Subtotal (Top 22 Products Account for 100% of Total)	2,363,674	
All Other	0	
Total	2,363,674	

* : Product for which the 2002 version of the HTS uses a somewhat different classification than was used in 2001.

Table A-9. Top 10 US imports from Chad, 2001

Actual dollars, customs value, imports for consumption

HTS Item and Description	Imports	NTR Tariff
Duty-Free on NTR Basis (98.7% of top 10 products)	**5,578,340**	
1301.20.00 Gum Arabic	4,452,005	Free
4407.29.00 Tropical wood sawn etc., over 6 mm thick	719,120	Free
4001.22.00 Technically specified natural rubber (TSNR)	172,035	Free
1302.20.00 Pectic substances, pectinates and pectates*	166,880	Free
4107.29.30 Reptile leather (other than vegetable pretanned), not fancy	42,900	Free
1301.90.90 Natural gums, resins, gum-resins etc.	20,900	Free
8542.13.80 Monolithic integrated circuits*	4,500	Free
Duty-Free For All GSP Countries (0.8% of top 10 products)	**46,083**	
8544.51.90 Insulated electric conductors (80V<V<1,000V)	46,083	2.6%
Duty-Free For LDC GSP Countries (0% of top 10 products)	**0**	
Duty-Free Only For AGOA Countries (0% of top 10 products)	**0**	
Textile & Apparel (0% of top 10 products)	**0**	
Special (0.5% of top 10 products)	**28,628**	
9999.95.00 Informal entries under $1251	19,865	
9801.00.10 US goods returned	8,763	
Subtotal (Top 10 Products Account for 100% of Total)	5,653,051	
All Other	0	
Total	5,653,051	

* : Product for which the 2002 version of the HTS uses a somewhat different classification than was used in 2001.

Table A-10. Top 7 US imports from Comoros, 2001

Actual dollars, customs value, imports for consumption

HTS Item and Description	Imports	NTR Tariff
Duty-Free on NTR Basis (99.7% of top 7 products)	**10,541,323**	
0905.00.00 Vanilla beans	9,644,654	Free
0907.00.00 Cloves (whole fruit, cloves and stems)	627,473	Free
3301.29.50 Essential oils (other than those of citrus fruits)	119,590	Free
0106.00.50 Live animals other than horses, asses, mules etc.*	94,716	Free
3302.90.10 Mixtures of or with a basis of odoriferous substances	48,802	Free
4901.99.00 Printed books, brochures, leaflets etc.	6,088	Free
Duty-Free For All GSP Countries (0% of top 7 products)	**0**	
Duty-Free For LDC GSP Countries (0% of top 7 products)	**0**	
Duty-Free Only For AGOA Countries (0% of top 7 products)	**0**	
Textile & Apparel (0% of top 7 products)	**0**	
Special (0.3% of top 7 products)	**26,757**	
9999.95.00 Informal entries under $1251	26,757	
Total	10,568,080	

* : Product for which the 2002 version of the HTS uses a somewhat different classification than was used in 2001.

Table A-11. Top 25 US imports from Congo (DROC), 2001

Thousands of dollars, customs value, imports for consumption

HTS Item and Description	Imports	NTR Tariff
Duty-Free on NTR Basis (19.5% of top 25 products)	**28,803**	
8105.10.60 Cobalt (other than alloy), unwrought*	11,105	Free
7102.31.00 Nonindustrial diamonds, unworked	9,610	Free
7108.12.10 Gold, nonmonetary, bullion and dore	2,575	Free
9706.00.00 Antiques of an age exceeding one hundred years	1,857	Free
7102.29.00 Industrial diamonds, worked, but not mounted or set	1,017	Free
4407.29.00 Tropical wood sawn etc., over 6 mm thick	524	Free
2615.90.60 Niobium, tantalum or vanadium ores etc.	503	Free
2302.30.00 Bran etc. from the sifting, milling of wheat	413	Free
4418.30.00 Wooden parquet panels	265	Free
8105.10.90 Cobalt, cobalt waste and scrap; cobalt powders*	256	Free
9705.00.00 Collections and collectors' pieces of zoological etc.	255	Free
3507.90.70 Enzymes and prepared enzymes	135	Free
4407.99.00 Nonconiferous woods sawn etc., over 6 mm thick	77	Free
8516.80.40 Electric heating resistors used for anti-icing or de-icing	51	Free
7102.21.30 Industrial diamonds (other than miner's diamonds)	47	Free
9015.80.80 Surveying, hydrographic etc. instruments and appliances	42	Free
9703.00.00 Original sculptures and statuary, in any material	34	Free
0301.10.00 Live ornamental fish	37	Free
Duty-Free For All GSP Countries (6.7% of top 25 products)	**9,840**	
7108.12.50 Gold, nonmonetary, unwrought	5,512	4.1%
7403.11.00 Refined copper cathodes and sections of cathodes	3,811	1.0%
1302.19.40 Ginseng (other than poppy straw extract)	517	1.0%
Duty-Free For LDC GSP Countries (73.7% of top 25 products)	**108,645**	
2709.00.20 Petroleum oils and oils from bituminous minerals	108,302	10.5¢/bbl.
8105.10.30 Cobalt alloy, unwrought*	343	4.4%
Duty-Free Only For AGOA Countries (0% of top 25 products)	**0**	
Textile & Apparel (0% of top 25 products)	**0**	
Special (0.08% of top 25 products)	**125**	
9999.95.00 Informal entries under $1251	93	
9801.00.10 US goods returned	32	
Subtotal (Top 25 Products Account for 99.8% of Total)	147,415	
All Other	299	
Total	147,713	

* : Product for which the 2002 version of the HTS uses a somewhat different classification than was used in 2001.

Table A-12. Top 25 US imports from Republic of Congo, 2001

Thousands of dollars, customs value, imports for consumption

HTS Item and Description	Imports	NTR Tariff
Duty-Free on NTR Basis (6.8% of top 25 products)	**30,973**	
7102.31.00 Nonindustrial diamonds, unworked	10,001	Free
2711.12.00 Propane, liquefied	9,634	Free
8105.10.60 Cobalt (other than alloy), unwrought	2,396	Free
2707.10.00 Benzene	1,650	Free
2711.29.00 Petroleum gases and other gaseous hydrocarbons	1,608	Free
2713.11.00 Coke, petroleum, not calcined	1,451	Free
1103.29.00 Cereal pellets except wheat*	729	Free
9706.00.00 Antiques of an age exceeding one hundred years	706	Free
2503.00.00 Sulfur of all kinds, other than sublimed sulfur etc.	630	Free
4408.39.00 Tropical wood, not over 6 mm thick	598	Free
7102.39.00 Nonindustrial diamonds, worked, but not mounted or set	559	Free
0901.11.00 Coffee, not roasted, not decaffeinated	375	Free
9705.00.00 Collections and collectors' pieces of zoological etc.	218	Free
2711.13.00 Butanes, liquefied	155	Free
7102.29.00 Industrial diamonds, worked, but not mounted or set	102	Free
2302.30.00 Bran etc. from the sifting, milling of wheat	89	Free
8471.49.10 Digital processing units	72	Free
Duty-Free For All GSP Countries (0.3% of top 25 products)	**1,385**	
7403.11.00 Refined copper cathodes and sections of cathodes	1,385	1.0%
Duty-Free For LDC GSP Countries (92.8% of top 25 products)	**424,311**	
2709.00.20 Petroleum oils and oils from bituminous minerals	307,707	10.5¢/bbl.
2710.00.05 Distillate and residual fuel oils from bitum. mins.*	86,362	5.25¢/bbl.
2709.00.10 Petroleum oils and oils from bitum. mins.	26,044	5.25¢/bbl.
2710.00.10 Distillate and residual fuel oils from bitum. mins.*	4,198	10.5¢/bbl.
Duty-Free Only For AGOA Countries (0.01% of top 25 products)	**66**	
9101.11.80 Wrist watches with cases of or clad with precious metal	66	[Complex]
Textile & Apparel (0% of top 25 products)	**0**	
Special (0.2% of top 25 products)	**747**	
9801.00.10 US goods returned	577	
9999.95.00 Informal entries under $1251	170	
Subtotal (Top 25 Products Account for 99.9% of Total)	457,478	
All Other	422	
Total	457,901	

* : Product for which the 2002 version of the HTS uses a somewhat different classification than was used in 2001.

Table A-13. Top 25 US imports from Cote d'Ivoire, 2001

Thousands of dollars, customs value, imports for consumption

HTS Item and Description	Imports	NTR Tariff
Duty-Free on NTR Basis (74.0% of top 25 products)	**231,926**	
1801.00.00 Cocoa beans, whole or broken, raw or roasted	206,034	Free
4407.29.00 Tropical wood sawn etc., over 6 mm thick	4,153	Free
0901.11.00 Coffee, not roasted, not decaffeinated	3,080	Free
1803.10.00 Cocoa paste, not defatted	2,689	Free
2713.11.00 Coke, petroleum, not calcined	2,080	Free
2711.29.00 Petroleum gases and other gaseous hydrocarbons	2,076	Free
8473.30.10 Parts & Accessories of computers, printed circuit assembles	1,689	Free
4408.39.00 Tropical wood, not over 6 mm thick	1,679	Free
4407.24.00 Virola, Mahogany, Imbuia and Balsa wood	1,602	Free
9705.00.00 Collections and collectors' pieces of zoological etc.	1,085	Free
4407.99.00 Nonconiferous woods sawn etc., over 6 mm thick	884	Free
2711.12.00 Propane, liquefied	868	Free
2902.70.00 Cumene	802	Free
9706.00.00 Antiques of an age exceeding one hundred years	777	Free
8473.30.50 Parts & Accessories of computers	708	Free
4408.90.00 Nontropical, nonconiferous veneer sheets etc.	688	Free
3203.00.10 Coloring matter of annato, archil, cochineal etc.	537	Free
2302.30.00 Bran etc. from the sifting, milling of wheat	495	Free
Duty-Free For All GSP Countries (4.2% of top 25 products)	**13,236**	
1803.20.00 Cocoa paste, wholly or partly defatted	5,655	0.2¢/kg.
1805.00.00 Cocoa powder, not containing added sugar	4,534	0.52¢/kg.
0802.90.94 Kola nuts, fresh or dried, shelled	3,047	5.0¢/kg.
Duty-Free For LDC GSP Countries (21.4% of top 25 products)	**67,015**	
2710.00.05 Distillate and residual fuel oils from bitum. mins.*	42,546	5.25¢/bbl.
2709.00.20 Petroleum oils and oils from bituminous minerals	20,330	10.5¢/bbl.
2710.00.10 Distillate and residual fuel oils from bitum. mins.*	4,139	10.5¢/bbl.
Duty-Free Only For AGOA Countries (0% of top 25 products)	**0**	
Textile & Apparel (0% of top 25 products)	**0**	
Special (0.4% of top 25 products)	**1,307**	
9801.00.10 US goods returned	1,307	
Subtotal (Top 25 Products Account for 98.0% of Total)	313,484	
All Other	6,339	
Total	319,823	

* : Product for which the 2002 version of the HTS uses a somewhat different classification than was used in 2001.

Table A-14. Top 8 US imports from Djibouti, 2001

Actual dollars, customs value, imports for consumption

HTS Item and Description	Imports	NTR Tariff
Duty-Free on NTR Basis (12.9% of top 8 products)	**122,673**	
2309.90.10 Mixed feed ingredients used in animal feeding	79,200	Free
1521.90.40 Insect waxes and spermaceti	36,900	Free
4907.00.00 Unused stamps of current or new issue in country	3,792	Free
8504.40.60 Power supplies for physical incorporation into computer	2,781	Free
Duty-Free For All GSP Countries (4.7% of top 8 products)	**44,692**	
3926.90.98 Articles of plastic	37,244	5.3%
8438.90.90 Parts of machinery for the industrial preparation etc.	7,448	2.8%
Duty-Free For LDC GSP Countries (0% of top 8 products)	**0**	
Duty-Free Only For AGOA Countries (0% of top 8 products)	**0**	
Textile & Apparel (0% of top 8 products)	**0**	
Special (82.4% of top 8 products)	**783,206**	
9801.00.10 US goods returned	777,905	
9999.95.00 Informal entries under $1251	5,301	
Total	950,571	

Table A-15. Top 14 US imports from Equatorial Guinea, 2001

Actual dollars, customs value, imports for consumption

HTS Item and Description	Imports	NTR Tariff
Duty-Free on NTR Basis (10.7% of top 14 products)	**42,156,448**	
2707.50.00 Aromatic hydrocarbon mixture	19,600,176	Free
2711.14.00 Ethylene, propylene, butylene and butadiene, liquefied	8,462,687	Free
2711.19.00 Liquefied petroleum gases and other gaseous hydrocarbons	8,181,481	Free
2901.22.00 Propene (Propylene)	3,833,962	Free
2711.29.00 Petroleum gases and other gaseous hydrocarbons	2,061,728	Free
4408.90.00 Nontropical, nonconiferous veneer sheets etc.	16,414	Free
Duty-Free For All GSP Countries (6.3% of top 14 products)	**24,959,859**	
2905.11.20 Methanol (Methyl alcohol)	24,953,905	8.0%
9027.10.60 Nonelectrical gas or smoke analysis apparatus	3,454	2.2%
9017.80.00 Instruments for measuring length, for use in the hand	2,500	5.3%
Duty-Free For LDC GSP Countries (82.2% of top 14 products)	**325,239,869**	
2709.00.20 Petroleum oils and oils from bituminous minerals	304,799,425	10.5¢/bbl.
2710.00.45 Mixture of hydrocarbons*	12,039,070	10.5¢/bbl.
2710.00.05 Distillate and residual fuel oils from bitum. mins.*	8,401,374	5.25¢/bbl.
Duty-Free Only For AGOA Countries (0% of top 14 products)	**0**	
Textile & Apparel (0% of top 14 products)	**0**	
Special (0.8% of top 14 products)	**3,252,928**	
9801.00.10 US goods returned	1,981,956	
9999.95.00 Informal entries under $1251	1,270,972	
Subtotal (Top 14 Products Account for 100% of Total)	395,609,104	
All Other	0	
Total	395,609,104	

* : Product for which the 2002 version of the HTS uses a somewhat different classification than was used in 2001.

Table A-16. Top 10 US imports from Eritrea, 2001

Actual dollars, customs value, imports for consumption

HTS Item and Description	Imports	NTR Tariff
Duty-Free on NTR Basis (60.0% of top 10 products)	**50,450**	
4102.21.00 Raw skins of sheep or lambs	35,806	Free
7118.10.00 Coin (other than gold coin), not being legal tender	12,285	Free
8481.90.90 Parts of taps, cocks, valves etc. for pipes, boiler shells	2,359	Free
Duty-Free on For All GSP Countries (42.6% of top 10 products)	**37,716**	
8544.41.80 Insulated electric conductors (<80V)	17,473	2.6%
9001.50.00 Spectacle lenses of materials other than glass, unmounted	4,900	2.0%
8708.94.50 Parts & Accessories of motor vehicle; steering wheels etc.	4,500	2.5%
3307.41.00 "Agarbatti" and other odoriferous preparations	4,426	2.4%
8302.30.30 Iron or steel, aluminum etc. for motor vehicles	4,249	2.0%
0603.10.80 Cut flowers and flower buds for bouquets, fresh cut	2,168	6.4%
Duty-Free on For LDC GSP Countries (0% of top 10 products)	**0**	
Duty-Free Only For AGOA Countries (0% of top 10 products)	**0**	
Textile & Apparel (0.5% of top 10 products)	**420**	
6109.10.00 T-shirts, singlets, etc. of cotton	420	17.4%
Special (0% of top 10 products)	**0**	
Subtotal (Top 10 Products Account for 100% of Total)	88,586	
All Other	0	
Total	88,586	

Table A-17. Top 25 US imports from Ethiopia, 2001

Actual dollars, customs value, imports for consumption

HTS Item and Description		Imports	NTR Tariff
Duty-Free on NTR Basis (94.2% of top 25 products)		**26,947,119**	
0901.11.00	Coffee, not roasted, not decaffeinated	10,450,720	Free
1207.99.00	Oil seeds and oleaginous fruits*	5,297,851	Free
1207.40.00	Sesame seeds, whether or not broken	3,899,136	Free
2309.90.10	Mixed feed ingredients used in animal feeding	3,777,983	Free
2615.90.60	Niobium, tantalum or vanadium ores etc.	1,910,700	Free
0901.12.00	Coffee, not roasted, decaffeinated	644,730	Free
1209.26.00	Timothy grass seed of a kind used for sowing	400,149	Free
1521.90.40	Insect waxes and spermaceti	177,566	Free
9706.00.00	Antiques of an age exceeding one hundred years	143,000	Free
1301.90.90	Natural gums, resins, gum-resins etc.	76,524	Free
2203.00.00	Beer made from malt	76,027	Free
8525.20.90	Transmission apparatus incorporating reception apparatus	52,733	Free
0909.40.00	Seeds of caraway	40,000	Free
Duty-Free For All GSP Countries (0.9% of top 25 products)		**270,240**	
1104.29.00	Grains of cereals other than barley, but not rolled	210,840	2.7%
0910.91.00	Mixtures of spices	59,400	1.9%
Duty-Free For LDC GSP Countries (0.8% of top 25 products)		**231,259**	
1403.10.00	Broomcorn of a kind used primarily in brooms or brushes*	116,169	$4.95/t
1008.20.00	Millet	58,000	0.32¢/kg.
1008.90.00	Cereals (including wild rice)	57,090	1.1%
Duty-Free Only For AGOA Countries (0% of top 25 products)		**0**	
Textile & Apparel (2.0% of top 25 products)		**573,587**	
5208.12.60	Woven cotton fabric, unbleached, of numbers 43-68	221,184	9.0%
6109.10.00	T-shirts, singlets, etc. of cotton	114,197	17.4%
6105.20.20	Men's or boys' shirts etc. of manmade fibers	104,249	32.5%
6302.91.00	Toilet and kitchen linen of cotton	81,289	9.5%
6110.30.30	Sweaters etc. of manmade fibers	52,668	32.4%
Special (2.0% of top 25 products)		**573,088**	
9801.00.10	US goods returned	371,601	
9802.00.50	Articles returned to the US	201,487	
Subtotal (Top 25 Products Account for 98.5% of Total)		28,595,293	
All Other		445,802	
Total		29,041,095	

* : Product for which the 2002 version of the HTS uses a somewhat different classification than was used in 2001.

Table A-18. Top 25 US imports from Gabon, 2001

Thousands of dollars, customs value, imports for consumption

HTS Item and Description	Imports	NTR Tariff
Duty-Free on NTR Basis (6.0% of top 25 products)	**103,454**	
2711.29.00 Petroleum gases and other gaseous hydrocarbons	24,133	Free
2602.00.00 Manganese ores and concentrates	21,586	Free
2713.11.00 Coke, petroleum, not calcined	14,250	Free
2707.10.00 Benzene	11,865	Free
2901.21.00 Ethylene	6,595	Free
2901.22.00 Propene (Propylene)	4,575	Free
2711.12.00 Propane, liquefied	4,045	Free
2503.00.00 Sulfur of all kinds, other than sublimed sulfur etc.	2,123	Free
4408.39.00 Tropical wood, not over 6 mm thick	2,096	Free
9706.00.00 Antiques of an age exceeding one hundred years	1,983	Free
4408.10.00 Coniferous veneer sheets and sheets etc.	1,660	Free
2901.24.10 Buta-l,3-diene	1,414	Free
2902.70.00 Cumene	1,410	Free
2902.30.00 Toluene	1,067	Free
4408.90.00 Nontropical, nonconiferous veneer sheets etc.	1,225	Free
9705.00.00 Collections and collectors' pieces of zoological etc.	1,008	Free
2901.10.10 Ethane and butane	1,002	Free
2302.30.00 Bran etc. from the sifting, milling of wheat	614	Free
2711.14.00 Ethylene, propylene, butylene and butadiene, liquefied	434	Free
2902.44.00 Mixed xylene isomers	369	Free
Duty-Free For All GSP Countries (0% of top 25 products)	**0**	
Duty-Free For LDC GSP Countries (94.0% of top 25 products)	**1,624,856**	
2709.00.20 Petroleum oils and oils from bituminous minerals	1,457,067	10.5¢/bbl.
2710.00.10 Distillate and residual fuel oils from bitum. mins.*	101,122	10.5¢/bbl.
2710.00.05 Distillate and residual fuel oils from bitum. mins.*	66,667	5.25¢/bbl.
Duty-Free Only For AGOA Countries (0% of top 25 products)	**0**	
Textile & Apparel (0% of top 25 products)	**0**	
Special (0.1% of top 25 products)	**2,365**	
9801.00.10 US goods returned	1,845	
9999.95.00 Informal entries under $1251	520	
Subtotal (Top 25 Products Account for 99.9% of Total)	1,730,673	
All Other	998	
Total	1,731,671	

* : Product for which the 2002 version of the HTS uses a somewhat different classification than was used in 2001.

Table A-19. Top 20 US imports from The Gambia, 2001

Actual dollars, customs value, imports for consumption

HTS Item and Description	Imports	NTR Tariff
Duty-Free on NTR Basis (49.2% of top 20 products)	**114,341**	
0306.13.00 Shrimps and prawns, dried, salted, frozen	105,936	Free
8424.90.90 Parts of mechanical appliances for projecting liquids etc.	5,711	Free
4907.00.00 Unused stamps of current or new issue in country	2,694	Free
Duty-Free For All GSP Countries (9.6% of top 20 products)	**22,197**	
9031.80.80 Measuring and checking instruments	22,197	1.7%
Duty-Free For LDC GSP Countries (12.1% of top 20 products)	**28,215**	
1202.20.40 Peanuts (ground-nuts), shelled	28,215	6.6¢/kg.
Duty-Free Only For AGOA Countries (0% of top 20 products)	**0**	
Textile & Apparel (27.9% of top 20 products)	**64,736**	
5208.31.60 Dyed plain weave fabrics of cotton of numbers 43-68	26,100	10.0%
5209.11.00 Unbleached plain weave fabrics of cotton	11,310	6.5%
6204.42.30 Women's or girls' dresses of cotton	10,223	9.2%
5208.52.40 Printed plain weave fabrics of cotton of numbers 43-68	7,760	11.4%
6206.30.30 Women's or girls' blouses etc. of cotton	1,640	15.6%
6304.92.00 Furnishing articles of cotton	1,600	6.5%
6104.42.00 Women's or girls' dresses of cotton	1,332	11.6%
6204.62.40 Women's or girls' trousers etc. of cotton	1,100	16.8%
6211.42.00 Women's or girls' track suits etc. of cotton	840	8.2%
6307.90.99 National flags etc. of textile materials*	821	7.0%
6204.52.20 Women's or girls' skirts etc. of cotton	650	8.3%
6204.12.00 Women's or girls' suits etc. of cotton	600	15.3%
5209.31.60 Dyed, plain weave fabrics of cotton	400	8.5%
6203.12.20 Men's or boys' suits of synthetic fibers	360	27.6%
Special (1.2% of top 20 products)	**2,864**	
9999.95.00 Informal entries under $1251	2,864	
Subtotal (Top 20 Products Account for 100% of Total)	232,353	
All Other	0	
Total	232,353	

Table A-20. Top 25 US imports from Ghana, 2001

Thousands of dollars, customs value, imports for consumption

HTS Item and Description	Imports	NTR Tariff
Duty-Free on NTR Basis (61.6% of top 25 products)	**109,923**	
1801.00.00 Cocoa beans, whole or broken, raw or roasted	39,652	Free
7601.10.60 Aluminum (other than alloy), unwrought	18,498	Free
4408.90.00 Nontropical, nonconiferous veneer sheets etc.	11,687	Free
1803.10.00 Cocoa paste, not defatted	6,792	Free
1804.00.00 Cocoa butter, fat and oil	6,761	Free
7601.20.90 Aluminum alloys, unwrought	5,381	Free
4407.29.00 Tropical wood sawn etc., over 6 mm thick	4,215	Free
4408.39.00 Tropical wood, not over 6 mm thick	3,930	Free
7102.31.00 Nonindustrial diamonds, unworked	3,311	Free
4407.99.00 Nonconiferous woods sawn etc., over 6 mm thick	2,201	Free
4407.24.00 Virola, Mahogany, Imbuia and Balsa wood	1,878	Free
7102.29.00 Industrial diamonds, worked, but not mounted or set	1,385	Free
7602.00.00 Aluminum, waste and scrap	1,264	Free
2620.90.60 Materials (ash and residues)*	1,220	Free
1802.00.00 Cocoa shells, husks, skins and other cocoa waste	769	Free
7108.11.00 Gold powder	508	Free
2302.30.00 Bran etc. from the sifting, milling of wheat	471	Free
Duty-Free For All GSP Countries (4.3% of top 25 products)	**7,691**	
4420.10.00 Wooden statuettes and other wood ornaments	2,442	3.2%
4412.13.50 Plywood, not over 6 mm thick, tropical wood*	1,720	8.0%
4412.14.30 Plywood, not over 6 mm thick, nontropical hardwood*	1,624	8.0%
0714.90.20 Fresh or chilled yams	1,112	6.4%
4412.13.40 Plywood sheets not over 6 mm thick, specified tropical wood	793	8.0%
Duty-Free For LDC GSP Countries (31.4% of top 25 products)	**56,040**	
2710.00.05 Distillate and residual fuel oils from bitum. mins.	37,953	5.25¢/bbl.
2710.00.25 Naphthas from petro oils & bitum. mins.*	18,087	10.5¢/bbl.
Duty-Free Only For AGOA (0% of top 25 products)	**0**	
Textile & Apparel (0% of top 25 products)	**0**	
Special (2.6% of top 25 products)	**4,689**	
9801.00.10 US goods returned	4,689	
Subtotal (Top 25 Products Account for 96.2% of Total)	178,340	
All Other	7,052	
Total	185,391	

* : Product for which the 2002 version of the HTS uses a somewhat different classification than was used in 2001.

Table A-21. Top 25 US imports from Guinea, 2001

Actual dollars, customs value, imports for consumption

HTS Item and Description	Imports	NTR Tariff
Duty-Free on NTR Basis (98.3% of top 25 products)	**86,105,404**	
2606.00.00 Aluminum ores and concentrates	68,170,532	Free
7102.31.00 Nonindustrial diamonds, unworked	13,707,481	Free
0901.11.00 Coffee, not roasted, not decaffeinated	3,103,792	Free
9706.00.00 Antiques of an age exceeding one hundred years	411,447	Free
7102.39.00 Nonindustrial diamonds, worked, but not mounted or set	235,089	Free
2302.30.00 Bran etc. from the sifting, milling of wheat	114,684	Free
0901.12.00 Coffee, not roasted, decaffeinated	91,270	Free
1511.90.00 Palm oil	78,467	Free
9705.00.00 Collections and collectors' pieces of zoological etc.	59,233	Free
1905.90.10 Bread, pastry, cake, biscuit etc.	47,842	Free
4407.29.00 Tropical wood sawn etc., over 6 mm thick	37,430	Free
1905.30.00 Sweet biscuits (pastry); waffles and wafers*	24,077	Free
8208.10.00 Knives and cutting blades for metal working machines etc.	24,060	Free
Duty-Free For All GSP Countries (0.6% of top 25 products)	**538,317**	
4810.21.00 Light-weight coated paper for graphic use*	238,305	0.5%
4420.10.00 Wooden statuettes and other wood ornaments	115,002	3.2%
9206.00.20 Percussion musical instruments; drums	49,530	4.8%
8411.99.90 Parts of gas turbines	48,823	2.4%
8408.20.20 Compression-ignition internal-combustion piston engines	39,000	2.5%
8543.89.96 Electrical machines and apparatus	25,157	2.6%
8481.80.90 Taps, cocks, valves appliances for pipes etc.	22,500	2.0%
Duty-Free For LDC GSP Countries (0.03% of top 25 products)	**22,638**	
1604.14.30 Tunas and skipjack, not in oil, in airtight containers	22,638	12.5%
Duty-Free Only For AGOA Countries (0% of top 25 products)	**0**	
Textile & Apparel (0.03% of top 25 products)	**26,210**	
6110.10.10 Sweaters etc., wholly of cashmere*	26,210	4.7%
Special (1.1% of top 25 products)	**936,558**	
9801.00.10 US goods returned	608,695	
9999.95.00 Informal entries under $1251	280,706	
9810.00.70 Wild animals imported	47,157	
Subtotal (Top 25 Products Account for 99.8 % of Total)	87,629,127	
All Other	203,126	
Total	87,832,253	

* : Product for which the 2002 version of the HTS uses a somewhat different classification than was used in 2001.

Table A-22. Top 2 US imports from Guinea-Bissau, 2001

Actual dollars, customs value, imports for consumption

HTS Item and Description	Imports	NTR Tariff
Duty-Free on NTR Basis (100% of top 2 products)	**18,933**	
4907.00.00 Unused stamps of current or new issue in country	16,066	Free
0301.10.00 Live ornamental fish	2,867	Free
Duty-Free For All GSP Countries (0% of top 2 products)	**0**	
Duty-Free For LDC GSP Countries (0% of top 2 products)	**0**	
Duty-Free Only For AGOA Countries (0% of top 2 products)	**0**	
Textile & Apparel (0% of top 2 products)	**0**	
Special (0% of top 2 products)	**0**	
Total	18,933	

* : Product for which the 2002 version of the HTS uses a somewhat different classification than was used in 2001.

Table A-23. Top 25 US imports from Kenya, 2001

Thousands of dollars, customs value, imports for consumption

HTS Item and Description	Imports	NTR Tariff
Duty-Free on NTR Basis (36.2% of top 25 products)	**41,316**	
0901.11.00 Coffee, not roasted, not decaffeinated	12,007	Free
0902.40.00 Black tea (fermented) and partly fermented tea	11,501	Free
1302.14.00 Saps and extracts of pyrethrum etc.	7,891	Free
2101.20.20 Extracts, essences or concentrates of tea or mate	2,608	Free
0304.20.60 Frozen fillets of fresh-water fish, flat fish, etc.	1,543	Free
8524.31.00 Pre-recorded discs for laser reading systems	1,375	Free
3203.00.10 Coloring matter of annato, archil, cochineal etc.	1,217	Free
8525.20.90 Transmission apparatus incorporating reception apparatus	823	Free
9706.00.00 Antiques of an age exceeding one hundred years	690	Free
8542.13.80 Monolithic integrated circuits*	576	Free
0901.12.00 Coffee, not roasted, decaffeinated	567	Free
8524.39.40 Recorded discs for laser system etc.; propietary media	518	Free
Duty-Free For All GSP Countries (1.7% of top 25 products)	**1,916**	
4420.10.00 Wooden statuettes and other wood ornaments	1,916	3.2%
Duty-Free For LDC GSP Countries (4.0% of top 25 products)	**4,583**	
2401.20.85 Tobacco, partly or wholly stemmed/stripped	1,657	37.5¢/kg.
3808.10.50 Insecticides for retail sale or as preparations or articles	1,266	5.0%
9507.90.70 Artificial baits and flies	1,026	9.0%
0802.90.98 Nuts, fresh or dried, shelled	634	5.0¢/kg.
Duty-Free Only For AGOA Countries (0% of top 25 products)	**0**	
Textile & Apparel (53.7% of top 25 products)	**61,372**	
6204.62.40 Women's or girls' trousers etc. of cotton	36,664	16.8%
6203.42.40 Men's or boys' trousers and shorts of cotton	20,128	16.8%
6205.20.20 Men's or boys' shirts of cotton	2,437	20.0%
6205.30.20 Men's or boys' shirts of manmade fibers	1,036	[Complex]
6208.92.00 Women's or girls' singlets etc. of man-made fibers	591	16.2%
6204.42.30 Women's or girls' dresses of cotton	516	9.2%
Special (4.4% of top 25 products)	**5,035**	
9801.00.10 US goods returned	4,300	
9999.95.00 Informal entries under $1251	735	
Subtotal (Top 25 Products Account for 88.8% of Total)	114,220	
All Other	14,362	
Total	128,582	

* : Product for which the 2002 version of the HTS uses a somewhat different classification than was used in 2001.

Table A-24. Top 25 US imports from Lesotho, 2001

Thousands of dollars, customs value, imports for consumption

HTS Item and Description		Imports	NTR Tariff
Duty-Free on NTR Basis (0% of top 25 Products)		**0**	
Duty-Free For All GSP Countries (0% of top 25 Products)		**0**	
Duty-Free For LDC GSP Countries (0% of top 25 Products)		**0**	
Duty-Free Only For AGOA Countries (0% of top 25 Products)		**0**	
Textile & Apparel (100% of top 25 Products)		**216,193**	
6110.20.20	Sweaters etc. of cotton	62,213	17.3%
6204.62.40	Women's or girls' trousers etc. of cotton	52,956	16.8%
6203.42.40	Men's or boys' trousers and shorts of cotton	45,852	16.8%
6104.62.20	Women's or girls' trousers etc. of cotton	8,216	15.3%
6105.10.00	Men's or boys' shirts of cotton	7,311	20.0%
6106.10.00	Women's or girls' blouses and shirts of cotton	7,269	20.0%
6110.30.30	Sweaters etc. of manmade fibers	7,157	32.4%
6109.10.00	T-shirts, singlets etc. of cotton	6,445	17.4%
6104.63.20	Women's or girls' trousers etc. of synthetic fibers	6,008	28.6%
6103.42.10	Men's or boys' trousers etc. of cotton	3,827	16.3%
6103.43.15	Men's or boys' trousers etc. of synthetic fibers	2,294	28.6%
6109.90.10	T-shirts, singlets etc. of man-made fibers	1,633	32.4%
6114.20.00	Garments of cotton	1,260	10.9%
6105.20.20	Men's or boys' shirts of manmade fibers	753	32.5%
6106.20.20	Women's or girls' blouses etc. of man-made fibers	494	32.5%
6112.12.00	Track suits of synthetic fibers	414	28.6%
6204.63.35	Women's or girls' trousers etc. of synthetic fibers	352	29.0%
6206.30.30	Women's or girls' blouses and shirts of cotton	316	15.6%
6203.43.40	Men's or boys' trousers etc. of synthetic fibers	307	28.3%
6104.53.20	Women's or girls' skirts etc. of synthetic fibers	251	16.2%
6211.11.10	Men's or boys' swimwear of man-made fibers	200	28.2%
6111.20.60	Babies' garments and clothing accessories of cotton	188	8.2%
6108.91.00	Women's or girls' negligees etc. of cotton	176	8.6%
6104.42.00	Women's or girls' dresses of cotton	157	11.6%
6111.20.50	Babies' trousers etc. of cotton	144	15.3%
Special (0% of top 25 Products)		**0**	
Subtotal (Top 25 Products Account for 99.6% of Total)		216,193	
All Other		973	
Total		217,165	

Table A-25. Top 25 US imports from Liberia, 2001

Actual dollars, customs value, imports for consumption

HTS Item and Description	Imports	NTR Tariff
Duty-Free on NTR Basis (98.2% of top 25 products)	**41,799,954**	
4001.10.00 Natural rubber latex, whether or not prevulcanized	41,153,874	Free
9503.80.00 Toys and motors, incorporating a motor etc.	160,112	Free
4407.99.00 Nonconiferous woods sawn etc., over 6 mm thick	84,569	Free
9706.00.00 Antiques of an age exceeding one hundred years	81,565	Free
8473.30.90 Parts & accessories of computers	73,248	Free
4901.99.00 Printed books, brochures, leaflets etc.	57,653	Free
8542.13.80 Monolithic integrated circuits*	57,010	Free
7018.10.50 Glass beads (other than imitation pearls)	51,098	Free
9705.00.00 Collections and collectors' pieces of zoological etc.	46,466	Free
1511.90.00 Palm oil	14,200	Free
7108.11.00 Gold powder	8,650	Free
8306.29.00 Base metal statuettes and other ornaments	4,000	Free
1513.29.00 Palm kernel oil	3,865	Free
8305.20.00 Base metal staples in strips	3,644	Free
Duty-Free For All GSP Countries (0.1% of top 25 products)	**56,026**	
8504.40.95 Static converters (for example, rectifiers)	48,682	1.5%
4011.20.50 New pneumatic tires of rubber etc. (excluding radials)	4,500	3.4%
8501.10.40 Electric motors of an output of under 18.65 W	2,844	4.4%
Duty-Free For LDC GSP Countries (0.06% of top 25 products)	**26,331**	
7317.00.55 Iron or steel etc., made of round wire	24,326	0.1%
8483.30.80 Bearing housings; plain shaft bearings	2,005	4.5%
Duty-Free Only For AGOA Countries (0% of top 25 products)	**0**	
Textile & Apparel (0.08% of top 25 products)	**32,432**	
6704.19.00 Wigs (partial) etc. of synthetic textile materials	29,283	Free
6302.31.70 Bed linen, of cotton	1,407	4.6%
6204.42.30 Women's or girls' dresses of cotton	1,404	9.2%
5209.59.00 Printed woven fabrics of cotton	338	8.5%
Special (1.5% of top 25 products)	**643,451**	
9801.00.10 US goods returned	637,569	
9999.95.00 Informal entries under $1251	5,882	
Subtotal (Top 25 Products Account for 100% of Total)	42,558,194	
All Other	0	
Total	42,558,194	

* : Product for which the 2002 version of the HTS uses a somewhat different classification than was used in 2001.

Table A-26. Top 25 US imports from Madagascar, 2001

Thousands of dollars, customs value, imports for consumption

HTS Item and Description	Imports	NTR Tariff
Duty-Free on NTR Basis (32.6% of top 25 products)	**83,368**	
0905.00.00 Vanilla beans	75,517	Free
9706.00.00 Antiques of an age exceeding one hundred years	1,508	Free
2504.10.50 Natural graphite in powder (other than crystalline flake)	1,176	Free
3301.29.50 Essential oils (other than those of citrus fruits)	1,052	Free
0907.00.00 Cloves (whole fruit, cloves and stems)	2,517	Free
0901.11.00 Coffee, not roasted, not decaffeinated	1,598	Free
Duty-Free For All GSP Countries (0.9% of top 25 products)	**2,355**	
1701.11.10 Cane sugar, raw, in solid form	2,355	[Complex]
Duty-Free For LDC GSP Countries (0% of top 25 products)	**0**	
Duty-Free Only For AGOA Countries (0% of top 25 products)	**0**	
Textile & Apparel (66.4% of top 25 products)	**169,646**	
6110.20.20 Sweaters etc. of cotton	40,756	17.3%
6203.42.40 Men's or boys' trousers and shorts of cotton	27,977	16.8%
6204.62.40 Women's or girls' trousers etc. of cotton	24,931	16.8%
6110.10.10 Sweaters etc. wholly of cashmere*	20,652	4.7%
6205.20.20 Men's or boys' shirts of cotton	12,221	20.0%
6110.10.20 Sweaters etc. of wool or fine animal hair*	9,075	16.2%
6109.10.00 T-shirts, singlets etc. of cotton	5,534	17.4%
6110.30.15 Sweaters etc. of manmade fibers	4,828	17.0%
6110.30.30 Sweaters etc. of manmade fibers	4,263	32.4%
6108.91.00 Women's or girls' negligees etc. of cotton	3,694	8.6%
6104.62.20 Women's or girls' trousers etc. of cotton	2,859	15.3%
6108.21.00 Women's or girls' briefs and panties of cotton	2,319	7.7%
6103.43.15 Men's or boys' trousers etc. of synthetic fibers	2,250	28.6%
6106.10.00 Women's or girls' blouses and shirts of cotton	2,240	20.0%
6103.42.10 Men's or boys' trousers etc. of cotton	1,930	16.3%
6114.20.00 Garments of cotton	1,503	10.9%
6105.10.00 Men's or boys' shirts of cotton	1,432	20.0%
6209.20.30 Babies' trousers etc. of cotton	1,182	15.5%
Special (0% of top 25 products)	**0**	
Subtotal (Top 25 Products Account for 94.0%)	255,369	
All Other	16,423	
Total	271,791	

* : Product for which the 2002 version of the HTS uses a somewhat different classification than was used in 2001.

Table A-27. Top 25 US imports from Malawi, 2001

Actual dollars, customs value, imports for consumption

HTS Item and Description	Imports	NTR Tariff
Duty-Free on NTR Basis (18.8% of top 25 products)	**13,446,491**	
0902.40.00 Black tea (fermented) and partly fermented tea	12,601,169	Free
2401.30.23 Tobacco refuse, other than for cigarettes	586,633	Free
0902.20.90 Green tea in packages over 3 kg, not flavored	169,727	Free
0901.11.00 Coffee, not roasted, not decaffeinated	57,983	Free
0301.10.00 Live ornamental fish	30,979	Free
Duty-Free For All GSP Countries (11.2% of top 25 products)	**8,007,259**	
1701.11.10 Cane sugar, raw, in solid form	7,823,159	[complex]
0904.20.60 Fruits of the genus Capsicum, not ground	104,706	2.5¢/kg.
0713.39.40 Dried beans, shelled Sept.1-April 30	79,394	0.8¢/kg.
Duty-Free For LDC GSP Countries (52.8% of top 25 products)	**37,779,933**	
2401.20.85 Tobacco, partly or wholly stemmed/stripped	20,689,113	37.5¢/kg.
2401.20.83 Tobacco, partly or wholly stemmed/stripped	16,373,812	37.5¢/kg.
0802.90.98 Nuts, fresh or dried, shelled	717,008	5.0¢/kg.
Duty-Free Only For AGOA Countries (0% of top 25 products)	**0**	
Textile & Apparel (17.1% of top 25 products)	**12,219,314**	
6105.10.00 Men's or boys' shirts of cotton	2,292,760	20.0%
6203.42.40 Men's or boys' trousers and shorts of cotton	2,876,393	[complex]
6201.92.20 Men's or boys' anoraks, windbreakers etc.	1,680,876	9.5%
6205.20.20 Men's or boys' shirts of cotton	1,192,871	20.0%
6204.62.40 Women's or girls' trousers etc. of cotton	850,746	16.8%
6204.63.35 Women's or girls' trousers etc. of synthetic fibers	748,779	29.0%
6203.43.40 Men's or boys' trousers etc. of synthetic fibers	731,564	28.3%
6110.20.20 Sweaters etc. of cotton	562,977	17.3%
6110.30.30 Sweaters etc. of manmade fibers	441,572	32.4%
6210.40.50 Men's or boys' garments	322,152	7.2%
6205.30.20 Men's or boys' shirts of manmade fibers	269,452	[complex]
6103.43.15 Men's or boys' trousers etc. of synthetic fibers	160,787	28.6%
6109.10.00 T-shirts, singlets, etc. of cotton	88,385	17.4%
Special (0.05% of top 25 products)	**39,223**	
9999.95.00 Informal entries under $1251	39,223	
Subtotal (Top 25 Products Account for 99.6% of Total)	71,492,220	
All other	308,114	
Total	71,800,334	

Table A-28. Top 25 US imports from Mali, 2001

Actual dollars, customs value, imports for consumption

HTS Item and Description	Imports	NTR Tariff
Duty-Free on NTR Basis (52.4% of top 25 products)	**3,044,717**	
9503.70.00 Toys, put up in sets or outfits etc.	1,051,001	Free
9705.00.00 Collections and collectors' pieces of zoological etc.	452,207	Free
9706.00.00 Antiques of an age exceeding one hundred years	298,272	Free
7108.11.00 Gold powder	260,000	Free
0106.00.50 Live animals other than horses, asses, mules etc.*	166,899	Free
4102.29.00 Raw skins of sheep or lamb*	147,775	Free
4103.10.00 Raw hides and skins of goats or kids *	129,200	Free
8471.30.00 Portable digital automatic data processing machines*	107,459	Free
8471.80.10 Control or adapter units for computer	103,545	Free
4102.21.00 Raw skins of sheep or lambs	82,992	Free
8542.13.80 Monolithic digital integrated circuits*	59,882	Free
8536.90.40 Electrical terminals etc.	48,359	Free
4103.90.00 Raw hides and skins of animals*	47,344	Free
9401.69.60 Chairs with wooden frames (other than teak), not upholstered	46,782	Free
7108.12.10 Gold, nonmonetary, bullion and dore	43,000	Free
Duty-Free For All GSP Countries (6.3% of top 25 products)	**366,964**	
4420.10.00 Wooden statuettes and other wood ornaments	121,466	3.2%
4412.29.45 Plywood; surface covered other than clear	80,579	8.0%
7108.13.70 Gold, nonmonetary, in semimanufactured forms	55,783	4.1%
8536.50.40 Electrical motor starters (< 1,000 V)	47,961	2.7%
7117.90.90 Imitation jewelry not of base metal or plastics	23,500	11.0%
9028.90.00 Parts and accessories for gas, liquid etc.	37,675	3.2%
Duty-Free For LDC GSP Countries (0% of top 25 products)	**0**	
Duty-Free For AGOA Countries (0% of top 25 products)	**0**	
Textile & Apparel (0.8% of top 25 products)	**46,870**	
6304.92.00 Furnishing articles of cotton	46,870	6.5%
Special (40.5% of top 25 products)	**2,353,095**	
9801.00.10 US goods returned	1,598,336	
9999.95.00 Informal entries under $1251	654,521	
9812.00.20 Articles imported by certain organizations	100,238	
Subtotal (Top 25 Products Account for 93.7% of Total)	5,811,646	
All Other	393,730	
Total	6,205,376	

* : Product for which the 2002 version of the HTS uses a somewhat different classification than was used in 2001.

Table A-29. Top 10 US imports from Mauritania, 2001

Actual dollars, customs value, imports for consumption

HTS Item and Description	Imports	NTR Tariff
Duty-Free on NTR Basis (54.4% of top 10 products)	**159,589**	
8542.30.00 Monolithic integrated circuits*	115,463	Free
0307.59.00 Octopus, frozen, dried, salted	26,060	Free
8542.19.80 Monolithic digital integrated circuits*	6,450	Free
8471.41.00 Digital computers, nonportable over 10 kg	6,000	Free
8525.20.30 Transceivers for radiotelephony etc.	2,900	Free
9705.00.00 Collections and collectors' pieces of zoological etc.	2,078	Free
9505.90.60 Festive, carnival or other entertainment articles	638	Free
Duty-Free For All GSP Countries (0% of top 10 products)	**0**	
Duty-Free For LDC GSP Countries (12.8% of top 10 products)	**37,555**	
9507.10.00 Fishing rods and parts & accessories	37,555	6.0%
Duty-Free Only For AGOA Countries (0% of top 10 products)	**0**	
Textile & Apparel (0.3% of top 10 products)	**1,003**	
6214.90.00 Shawls etc. of textile materials	1,003	11.3%
Special (32.5% of top 10 products)	**95,392**	
9801.00.10 US goods returned	95,392	
Subtotal (Top 10 Products Account for 100% of Total)	293,539	
All Other	0	
Total	293,539	

* : Product for which the 2002 version of the HTS uses a somewhat different classification than was used in 2001.

Table A-30. Top 25 US imports from Mauritius, 2001

Thousands of dollars, customs value, imports for consumption

HTS Item and Description	Imports	NTR Tariff
Duty-Free on NTR Basis (5.1% of top 25 products)	**13,013**	
7102.39.00 Nonindustrial diamonds, worked, but not mounted or set	6,927	Free
0106.00.50 Live animals other than horses, asses, mules etc.*	3,280	Free
9706.00.00 Antiques of an age exceeding one hundred years	1,817	Free
3303.00.30 Perfumes and toilet waters, containing alcohol	989	Free
Duty-Free For All GSP Countries (5.1% of top 25 products)	**13,063**	
1701.11.10 Cane sugar, raw, in solid form	5,760	[Complex]
1703.90.50 Molasses	2,585	[Complex]
1703.10.50 Cane molasses	1,792	[Complex]
9004.10.00 Sunglasses, corrective, protective or other	1,637	2.0%
7113.11.20 Silver articles of jewelry valued not over $18/dozen pieces	1,289	13.5%
Duty-Free For LDC GSP Countries (0% of top 25 products)	**0**	
Duty-Free Only For AGOA Countries (0% of top 25 products)	**0**	
Textile & Apparel (88.4% of top 25 products)	**225,985**	
6203.42.40 Men's or boys' trousers and shorts of cotton	66,898	16.8%
6204.62.40 Women's or girls' trousers etc. of cotton	57,827	16.8%
6205.20.20 Men's or boys' shirts of cotton	42,731	20.0%
6110.20.20 Sweaters etc. of cotton	25,830	17.3%
6204.52.20 Women's or girls' skirts etc. of cotton	7,084	8.3%
6109.10.00 T-shirts, singlets etc. of cotton	5,297	17.4%
6110.10.20 Sweaters etc. of wool or fine animal hair	4,088	16.2%
6105.10.00 Men's or boys' shirts of cotton	3,665	20.0%
6104.62.20 Women's or girls' trousers etc. of cotton	3,157	15.3%
6110.30.30 Sweaters etc. of manmade fibers	2,904	32.4%
6106.20.20 Women's or girls' blouses and shirts of man-made fibers	1,814	32.5%
6106.10.00 Women's or girls' blouses and shirts of cotton	1,595	20.0%
6202.92.20 Women's or girls' anoraks etc. of cotton	1,248	9.0%
6204.42.30 Women's or girls' dresses of cotton	925	9.2%
6206.30.30 Women's or girls' blouses and shirts of cotton	922	15.6%
Special (1.4% of top 25 products)	**3,600**	
9801.00.10 US goods returned	3,600	
Subtotal (Top 25 Products Account for 92.9% of Total)	255,663	
All Other	19,464	
Total	275,127	

* : Product for which the 2002 version of the HTS uses a somewhat different classification than was used in 2001.

Table A-31. Top 25 US imports from Mozambique, 2001

Actual dollars, customs value, imports for consumption

HTS Item and Description	Imports	NTR Tariff
Duty-Free on NTR Basis (20.4% of top 25 products)	**1,437,088**	
0801.32.00 Cashew nuts, fresh or dried, shelled	1,090,211	Free
2008.19.10 Brazil nuts and cashew nuts	153,020	Free
0106.00.50 Live animals other than horses, asses, mules etc.*	96,758	Free
4407.10.00 Coniferous wood sawn etc. over 6 mm thick	36,972	Free
9705.00.00 Collections and collectors' pieces of zoological etc.	15,000	Free
9703.00.00 Original sculptures and statuary, in any material	12,700	Free
8542.13.80 Monolithic digital integrated circuits*	8,100	Free
4403.99.00 Wood in the rough	7,142	Free
4403.20.00 Coniferous wood in the rough	5,073	Free
9503.49.00 Toys or parts representing animals/non-human	4,638	Free
4907.00.00 Unused stamps of current or new issue in country	3,500	Free
6815.99.40 Articles of stone or of other mineral substances	2,340	Free
9505.10.15 Articles for Christmas festivities, ornaments of wood	1,634	Free
Duty-Free For All GSP Countries (74.8% of top 25 products)	**5,277,743**	
1701.11.10 Cane sugar, raw, in solid form	5,253,319	[Complex]
7325.99.50 Steel, cast articles	9,748	2.9%
6802.99.00 Monumental or building stone	6,595	6.5%
4420.10.00 Wooden statuettes and other wood ornaments	5,550	3.2%
4421.90.98 Articles of wood*	2,531	3.3%
Duty-Free For LDC GSP Countries (0% of top 25 products)	**0**	
Duty-Free Only For AGOA Countries (0% of top 25 products)	**0**	
Textile & Apparel (2.5% of top 25 products)	**179,179**	
6202.93.45 Women's or girls' anoraks etc. of manmade fibers	85,423	7.2%
6110.30.30 Sweaters etc. of manmade fibers	75,382	32.4%
6201.93.30 Men's or boys' anoraks etc. of manmade fibers	9,430	7.2%
6205.20.20 Men's or boys' shirts of cotton	8,944	20.0%
Special (2.3% of top 25 products)	**164,619**	
9801.00.10 US goods returned	95,350	
9999.95.00 Informal entries under $1251	45,229	
9801.00.25 Articles reimported	24,040	
Subtotal (Top 25 Products Account for 99.9% of Total)	7,058,629	
All Other	1,429	
Total	7,060,058	

* : Product for which the 2002 version of the HTS uses a somewhat different classification than was used in 2001.

Table A-32. Top 25 US imports from Namibia, 2001

Actual dollars, customs value, imports for consumption

HTS Item and Description	Imports	NTR Tariff
Duty-Free on NTR Basis (95.4% of top 25 products)	**35,917,623**	
7402.00.00 Unrefined copper	11,446,122	Free
2844.10.20 Natural uranium compounds	11,301,632	Free
0304.20.60 Frozen fillets of fresh-water fish, flat fish, etc.	9,959,713	Free
0304.20.50 Fillets and minced meat, frozen, of hake	1,699,555	Free
0306.11.00 Rock lobster, frozen	281,893	Free
0303.79.40 Fish, frozen	277,658	Free
7105.10.00 Diamond dust and powder	185,826	Free
7204.29.00 Alloy steel (other than stainless) waste and scrap	182,644	Free
7102.21.40 Industrial diamonds, unworked	136,794	Free
0304.20.20 Frozen fish fillets, skinned	89,734	Free
7102.29.00 Industrial diamonds, worked, but not mounted or set	84,520	Free
0302.69.20 Smelts, cusk, hake, etc.	74,211	Free
0302.32.00 Yellowfin tunas	30,471	Free
6815.99.40 Articles of stone or other mineral substances	30,115	Free
8431.31.00 Parts suitable for use solely with skip hoists or escalators	26,708	Free
9705.00.00 Collections and collectors' pieces of zoological etc.	24,467	Free
2203.00.00 Beer made from malt	23,760	Free
3101.00.00 Animal or vegetable fertilizers	22,580	Free
0302.39.00 Tunas except fillets, livers, roes etc.	20,720	Free
7108.11.00 Gold powder	18,500	Free
Duty-Free For All GSP Countries (0.2% of top 25 products)	**67,047**	
4420.10.00 Wooden statuettes and other wood ornaments	67,047	3.2%
Duty-Free For LDC GSP Countries (0% of top 25 products)	**0**	
Duty-Free Only For AGOA Countries (0% of top 25 products)	**0**	
Textile & Apparel (0.3% of top 25 products)	**95,325**	
6201.93.30 Men's or boys' anoraks etc. of manmade fibers	61,939	7.2%
6202.93.45 Women's or girls' anoraks etc. of manmade fibers	33,386	7.2%
Special (4.2% of top 25 products)	**1,571,463**	
9999.95.00 Informal entries under $1251	855,652	
9801.00.10 US goods returned	715,811	
Subtotal (Top 25 Products Account for 99.5% of Total)	37,651,458	
All Other	193,123	
Total	37,844,581	

Table A-33. Top 25 US imports from Niger, 2001

Actual dollars, customs value, imports for consumption

HTS Item and Description	Imports	NTR Tariff
Duty-Free on NTR Basis (28.0% of top 25 products)	**377,996**	
8471.70.60 Computer storage units	90,825	Free
9026.90.60 Parts & Accessories of nonelectrical instruments	71,161	Free
8412.21.00 Hydraulic power engines and motors, linear acting (cylinders)	64,000	Free
9018.90.80 Instrument used in medical, surgical, dental purposes	37,307	Free
9026.10.40 Flow meters for measuring the flow of liquids	35,263	Free
8479.90.95 Parts of machines having individual functions*	28,601	Free
8803.30.00 Parts of airplanes and helicopters	23,379	Free
3406.00.00 Candles, tapers	7,493	Free
3915.90.00 Waste, parings and scrap, of plastics	7,265	Free
8411.91.90 Parts of turbojets or turbopropellers	6,370	Free
0101.19.00 Live horses other than purebred breeding horses*	6,332	Free
Duty-Free For All GSP Countries (34.1% of top 25 products)	**465,907**	
4802.60.90 Paper and paperboard for graphic arts purposes*	261,183	0.6%
3920.62.00 Nonadhesive plates etc. of poly (ethylene terephthalate)	84,047	4.2%
3903.30.00 Acrylonitrile-butadiene-styrene copolymers, in primary forms	58,177	6.5%
2922.42.50 Glutamic acid and its salts, other than monosodium glutamate	29,134	3.7%
8483.40.90 Gears and gearing	19,823	2.5%
8409.91.50 Parts used solely with engines for vehicles	6,971	2.5%
4810.12.00 Paper or Paperboard for writing: over 150g/m2 etc.*	6,572	0.5%
Duty-Free For LDC GSP Countries (9.7% of top 25 products)	**132,313**	
8102.91.10 Molybdenum, unwrought*	107,514	[Complex]
7604.21.00 Aluminum alloy, hollow profiles	13,799	1.5%
3918.10.40 Wall or ceiling coverings of textile fibers, not man-made	11,000	5.3%
Duty-Free Only For AGOA Countries (0% of top 25 products)	**0**	
Textile & Apparel (3.5% of top 25 products)	**47,486**	
6214.20.00 Shawls etc. of wool or fine animal hair	30,453	6.7%
6301.20.00 Blankets etc. of wool or fine animal hair	17,033	[Complex]
Special (25.0% of top 25 products)	**341,639**	
9999.95.00 Informal entries under $1251	280,855	
9801.00.10 US goods returned	60,784	
Subtotal (Top 25 Products Account for 95.7% of Total)	1,365,341	
All Other	61,317	
Total	1,426,658	

* : Product for which the 2002 version of the HTS uses a somewhat different classification than was used in 2001.

Table A-34. Top 25 US imports from Nigeria, 2001

Thousands of dollars, customs value, imports for consumption

HTS Item and Description	Imports	NTR Tariff
Duty-Free on NTR Basis (10.9% of top 25 products)	**969,826**	
2713.11.00 Coke, petroleum, not calcined	206,594	Free
2711.11.00 Natural gas, liquefied	176,129	Free
2711.29.00 Petroleum gases and other gaseous hydrocarbons	151,084	Free
2711.12.00 Propane, liquefied	73,312	Free
2901.21.00 Ethylene	59,893	Free
2901.22.00 Propene (Propylene)	59,165	Free
2711.14.00 Ethylene etc., liquefied	32,373	Free
2711.13.00 Butanes, liquefied	30,393	Free
2902.44.00 Mixed xylene isomers	27,941	Free
2711.19.00 Liquefied petroleum gases and other gaseous hydrocarbons	24,380	Free
2902.20.00 Benzene	20,633	Free
2713.20.00 Petroleum bitumen	20,295	Free
2707.99.50 Products of hi-temp coal tar distillation etc.	15,612	Free
2902.70.00 Cumene	13,339	Free
2503.00.00 Sulfur of all kinds other than sublimed sulfur etc.	13,188	Free
2615.90.60 Niobium, tantalum or vanadium ores and concentrates	11,881	Free
2901.10.10 Ethane and butane	10,128	Free
2902.30.00 Toluene	9,567	Free
2901.24.10 Buta-l,3-diene	7,698	Free
2802.00.00 Sulfur, sublimed or precipitated; colloidal sulfur	6,221	Free
Duty-Free For All GSP Countries (0% of top 25 products)	**0**	
Duty-Free For LDC GSP Countries (89.1% of top 25 products)	**7,913,419**	
2709.00.20 Petroleum oils and oils from bituminous minerals	6,843,782	10.5¢/bbl.
2710.00.05 Distillate and residual fuel oils from bitum. mins.*	481,659	5.25¢/bbl.
2710.00.10 Distillate and residual fuel oils from bitum. mins.*	479,587	10.5¢/bbl.
2710.00.45 Mixture of hydrocarbons*	60,185	10.5¢/bbl.
2710.00.25 Naphthas from petro oils and bitum. mins.*	48,206	10.5¢/bbl.
Duty-Free Only For AGOA Countries (0% of top 25 products)	**0**	
Textile & Apparel (0% of top 25 products)	**0**	
Special (0% of top 25 products)	**0**	
Subtotal (Top 25 Products Account for 99.6% of Total)	8,883,245	
All Other	33,231	
Total	8,916,476	

* : Product for which the 2002 version of the HTS uses a somewhat different classification than was used in 2001.

Table A-35. Top 15 US imports from Rwanda, 2001

Actual dollars, customs value, imports for consumption

HTS Item and Description	Imports	NTR Tariff
Duty-Free on NTR Basis (94.1% of top 15 products)	**6,797,234**	
0901.11.00 Coffee, not roasted, not decaffeinated	3,667,510	Free
2615.90.60 Niobium, tantalum or vanadium ores etc.	3,101,332	Free
9701.10.00 Paintings, drawings and pastels	10,668	Free
9706.00.00 Antiques of an age exceeding one hundred years	8,500	Free
8534.00.00 Printed circuits, without elements	6,100	Free
8473.30.50 Parts & Accessories of computers	3,124	Free
Duty-Free For All GSP Countries (1.9% of top 15 products)	**138,045**	
9005.80.40 Optical telescopes, including monoculars	45,108	8.0%
2611.00.60 Tungsten concentrates	32,522	[Complex]
4420.10.00 Wooden statuettes and other wood ornaments	20,230	3.2%
3924.90.55 Household & toilet articles etc. of plastics	17,597	3.4%
9031.49.90 Optical measuring or checking instruments	11,411	3.5%
3920.10.00 Nonadhesive plates etc. of polymers of ethylene	11,177	4.2%
Duty-Free For LDC GSP Countries (3.7% of top 15 products)	**265,240**	
3808.10.50 Insecticides for retail sale or as preparations or articles	265,240	5.0%
Duty-Free Only For AGOA Countries (0% of top 15 products)	**0**	
Textile & Apparel (0.008% of top 15 products)	**613**	
4202.22.40 Handbags outer surface of textile materials	613	7.6%
Special (0.3% of top 15 products)	**19,739**	
9999.95.00 Informal entries under $1251	19,739	
Subtotal (Top 15 Products Account for 100% of Total)	7,220,871	
All Other	0	
Total	7,220,871	

Table A-36. Top 17 US imports from Sao Tome and Principe, 2001

Actual dollars, customs value, imports for consumption

HTS Item and Description	Imports	NTR Tariff
Duty-Free on NTR Basis (68.1% of top 17 products)	**219,590**	
8448.39.10 Parts of spinning, doubling or twisting machines	167,583	Free
8542.13.80 Monolithic digital integrated circuits*	17,347	Free
8431.39.00 Parts for use with lifting, handling machinery	15,066	Free
8473.30.90 Parts & Accessories of computers	9,730	Free
8413.60.00 Rotary positive displacement pumps for liquids	6,093	Free
8516.80.80 Electric heating resistors	3,771	Free
Duty-Free For All GSP Countries (21.3% of top 17 products)	**68,769**	
8477.90.85 Parts of machinery for working rubber or plastics etc.	49,851	3.1%
8537.10.90 Boards etc. equipped with apparatus for electric control	5,394	2.7%
7318.29.00 Iron or steel, nonthreaded articles etc.	5,319	2.8%
8481.20.00 Valves for oleohydraulic or pneumatic transmissions	4,502	2.0%
7326.90.85 Articles of Iron or steel	3,392	2.9%
3910.00.00 Silicones in primary forms	311	3.0%
Duty-Free For LDC GSP Countries (0% of top 17 products)	**0**	
Duty-Free Only For AGOA Countries (0% of top 17 products)	**0**	
Textile & Apparel (5.9% of top 17 products)	**18,897**	
5209.49.00 Woven fabrics of cotton of yarns of different colors	1,994	8.5%
5007.20.00 Woven fabrics of silk or of silk waste	16,269	Free
5910.00.90 Transmission etc. of textile materials	634	3.1%
Special (4.7% of top 17 products)	**15,050**	
9801.00.10 US goods returned	12,500	
9999.95.00 Informal entries under $1251	2,550	
Subtotal (Top 17 Products Account for 100% of Total)	322,306	
All Other	0	
Total	322,306	

* : Product for which the 2002 version of the HTS uses a somewhat different classification than was used in 2001.

Table A-37. Top 25 US imports from Senegal, 2001

Thousands of dollars, customs value, imports for consumption

HTS Item and Description	Imports	NTR Tariff
Duty-Free on NTR Basis (2.9% of top 25 products)	**2,953**	
8473.30.10 Parts & Accessories of computers, printed circuit assembles	841	Free
8525.40.40 Digital still image video cameras	661	Free
0302.69.40 Fish, excluding fillets, livers and roes, fresh or chilled etc.	634	Free
8471.70.40 Computer magnetic disk drive storage	321	Free
8471.50.00 Digital processing units	132	Free
9027.30.40 Electrical spectrometers, spectrophotometers etc.	115	Free
4906.00.00 Hand-drawn original plans and drawings	96	Free
0306.13.00 Shrimps and prawns, dried, salted, frozen	72	Free
0307.99.00 Molluscs etc. frozen, dried, salted	44	Free
1520.00.00 Glycerol, crude; glycerol waters and glycerol lyes	22	Free
0304.10.40 Fillets etc., fresh or chilled	15	Free
Duty-Free For All GSP Countries (1.1% of top 25 products)	**1,073**	
2905.45.00 Glycerol	434	0.5¢/kg.
9032.89.60 Automatic regulating instruments and apparatus	426	1.7%
9206.00.20 Percussion musical instruments; drums	97	4.8%
4420.10.00 Wooden statuettes and other wood ornaments	58	3.2%
8537.10.90 Boards etc. equipped with apparatus for electric control	40	2.7%
8536.50.90 Switches	18	2.7%
Duty-Free For LDC GSP Countries (5.4% of top 25 products)	**5,543**	
1508.10.00 Crude peanut (ground-nut) oil	5,543	7.5¢/kg.
Duty-Free Only For AGOA Countries (0% of top 25 products)	**0**	
Textile & Apparel (1.3% of top 25 products)	**1,279**	
6704.19.00 Wigs (partial) etc. of synthetic textile materials	1,127	Free
6703.00.60 Wool or other animal hair etc. for use in making wigs	64	Free
6704.11.00 Wigs (complete) of synthetic textile materials	36	Free
5208.52.40 Printed plain weave fabrics of cotton of number 43-68	30	11.4%
6704.90.00 Wigs, false beards etc. of animal hair or textile materials	22	Free
Special (89.4% of top 25 products)	**91,295**	
9801.00.10 US goods returned	84,358	
9999.95.00 Informal entries under $1251	6,937	
Subtotal (Top 25 Products Account for 99.8% of Total)	102,144	
All Other	201	
Total	102,345	

Table A-38. Top 25 US imports from Seychelles, 2001

Actual dollars, customs value, imports for consumption

HTS Item and Description	Imports	NTR Tariff
Duty-Free on NTR Basis (69.7% of top 25 products)	**16,527,722**	
0304.20.60 Frozen fillets of fresh-water fish, flat fish, etc.	14,279,390	Free
0303.79.40 Fish, frozen, excluding fillets etc.	1,075,866	Free
9030.40.00 Instruments & apparatus designed for telecommunications	375,632	Free
2504.90.00 Natural graphite, other than in powder or in flakes	354,718	Free
0303.77.00 Sea bass, frozen, excluding fillets	283,452	Free
8473.30.50 Parts & accessories of computer machines	44,620	Free
8545.90.40 Lamp carbons, battery carbons and articles of graphite etc.	25,994	Free
8471.41.00 Digital computer machines, nonportable or over 10 kg	13,528	Free
4407.10.00 Coniferous wood sawn etc. of a thickness exceeding 6 mm	13,155	Free
8542.13.80 Monolithic digital integrated circuits*	12,864	Free
8473.30.10 Parts & Accessories of computers, printed circuit assembles	11,000	Free
8542.50.00 Electronic microassemblies*	8,593	Free
4901.99.00 Printed books, brochures etc.	8,442	Free
9009.90.70 Parts and accessories of photocopying apparatus*	8,319	Free
9403.20.00 Furniture (other than seats) of metal	3,461	Free
4911.10.00 Printed trade advertising material, commercial catalogs	2,901	Free
9503.90.00 Toys, parts & accessories, reduced size	2,895	Free
9703.00.00 Original sculptures and statuary, in any material	2,892	Free
Duty-Free For All GSP Countries (18.7% of top 25 products)	**4,442,111**	
9020.00.90 Parts & accessories of breathing appliances & gas masks	4,405,500	2.5%
4203.30.00 Belts and bandoliers of leather or of composition leather	24,408	2.7%
8501.10.60 Electric motors (18.65W < W < 37.5W)	5,200	2.8%
8544.30.00 Insulated ignition wiring sets used in vehicles/aircraft/ships	4,428	5.0%
3707.90.32 Chemical preparations for photographic uses	2,575	6.5%
Duty-Free For LDC GSP Countries (0% of top 25 products)	**0**	
Duty-Free Only For AGOA Countries (0% of top 25 products)	**0**	
Textile & Apparel (0% of top 25 products)	**0**	
Special (11.5% of top 25 products)	**2,728,076**	
9999.95.00 Informal entries under $1251	2,042,495	
9801.00.10 US goods returned	685,581	
Subtotal (Top 25 Products Account for 99.9% of Total)	23,697,909	
All Other	2,856	
Total	23,700,765	

* : Product for which the 2002 version of the HTS uses a somewhat different classification than was used in 2001.

Table A-39. Top 25 US imports from Sierra Leone, 2001

Actual dollars, customs value, imports for consumption

HTS Item and Description	Imports	NTR Tariff
Duty-Free on NTR Basis (30.4% of top 25 products)	**1,086,886**	
9401.90.40 Parts of seats, of wood	230,203	Free
2941.90.50 Antibiotics other than aromatic or modified aromatic antibiotics	207,498	Free
7102.21.10 Miners' diamonds, unworked	152,708	Free
9403.90.70 Parts of furniture of wood	121,147	Free
7102.31.00 Nonindustrial diamonds, unworked	80,882	Free
2302.30.00 Bran etc. from the sifting, milling of wheat	80,752	Free
9401.90.10 Parts of seats, for seats of a kind used for motor vehicles	75,744	Free
9403.60.80 Furniture of wooden	73,039	Free
1511.90.00 Palm oil	64,913	Free
Duty-Free For All GSP Countries (19.4% of top 25 products)	**693,672**	
8302.10.60 Iron, aluminum, etc. parts, not designed for motor vehicles	195,860	3.5%
3908.10.00 Polyamide	153,530	6.3%
8411.99.90 Parts of gas turbines	101,500	2.4%
9008.30.00 Image projectors, other than cinematographic	94,630	4.6%
4013.90.50 Inner tubes of rubber for vehicles	81,535	3.7%
8708.29.50 Parts & Accessories of bodies for motor vehicles	66,617	2.5%
Duty-Free For LDC GSP Countries (0% of top 25 products)	**0**	
Duty-Free Only For AGOA Countries (0% of top 25 products)	**0**	
Textile & Apparel (50.3% of top 25 products)	**1,799,063**	
6204.11.00 Women's or girls' suits of wool or fine animal hair	359,563	14.6%
6403.99.60 Footwear with outer soles of rubber etc. not covering the ankle	357,473	8.5%
6403.91.60 Footwear with outer soles of rubber etc. covering the ankle	345,139	8.5%
6204.31.20 Women's or girls' suit-type jackets of wool or fine animal hair	187,800	[Complex]
6403.99.90 Footwear valued over $2.50/pair tennis; not for women	148,553	10.0%
6206.10.00 Women's or girls' blouses etc. of silk or silk waste	126,147	7.0%
6204.19.20 Women's or girls' suits, of artificial fibers	71,188	[Complex]
4203.10.40 Articles of apparel, of leather or of composition leather	70,831	6.0%
6202.11.00 Women's or girls' overcoats etc. of wool or fine animal hair	70,819	[Complex]
6204.51.00 Women's or girls' skirts etc. of wool or fine animal hair	61,550	14.6%
Special (0% of top 25 products)	**0**	
Subtotal (Top 25 Products Account for 77.1% of Total)	3,579,621	
All Other	1,060,842	
Total	4,640,463	

* : Product for which the 2002 version of the HTS uses a somewhat different classification than was used in 2001.

Table A-40. Top 16 US imports from Somalia, 2001

Actual dollars, customs value, imports for consumption

HTS Item and Description	Imports	NTR Tariff
Duty-Free on NTR Basis (62.2% of top 16 products)	**213,556**	
3301.29.50 Essential oils (other than those of citrus fruits)	151,096	Free
1301.90.90 Natural gums, resins, gum-resins etc.	25,934	Free
2701.19.00 Coal, other than anthracite, but not agglomerated	12,000	Free
8512.90.60 Parts of electrical lighting equipment for motor vehicles	8,037	Free
4907.00.00 Unused stamps of current or new issue in country	5,000	Free
2508.10.00 Bentonite clay, whether or not calcined	3,401	Free
8524.39.40 Recorded discs for laser system; propietary media	3,010	Free
7118.10.00 Coin (other than gold coin), not being legal tender	2,880	Free
9403.50.90 Furniture (other than seats) of wood (other than bentwood)	2,198	Free
Duty-Free For All GSP Countries (0% of top 16 products)	**0**	
Duty-Free For LDC GSP Countries (17.6% of top 16 products)	**60,293**	
2401.20.83 Tobacco, partly or wholly stemmed/stripped	55,943	37.5¢/kg.
8504.40.95 Static converters (for example, rectifiers)	4,350	1.5%
Duty-Free Only For AGOA Countries (0% of top 16 products)	**0**	
Textile & Apparel (20.1% of top 16 products)	**69,076**	
6110.10.10 Sweaters etc. wholly of cashmere*	50,874	4.7%
6204.62.40 Women's or girls' trousers etc. of cotton	16,823	16.8%
6203.39.90 Men's or boys' suit-type jackets etc. of text materials	1,029	6.6%
5007.90.60 Silk woven fabrics of silk	350	4.7%
Special (0.1% of top 16 products)	**370**	
9999.95.00 Informal entries under $1251	370	
Subtotal (Top 16 Products Account for 100% of Total)	343,295	
All Other	0	
Total	343,295	

* : Product for which the 2002 version of the HTS uses a somewhat different classification than was used in 2001.

Table A-41. Top 25 US imports from South Africa, 2001

Thousands of dollars, customs value, imports for consumption

HTS Item and Description	Imports	NTR Tariff
Duty-Free on an NTR Basis (78.3% of Top 25 Products)	**2,491,847**	
7110.11.00 Platinum, unwrought or in powder form	802,298	Free
7110.21.00 Palladium, unwrought or in powder form	403,802	Free
7102.31.00 Nonindustrial diamonds, unworked or simply sawn	289,641	Free
7110.31.00 Rhodium, unwrought or in powder form	217,579	Free
8421.39.40 Catalytic converters	165,775	Free
7102.39.00 Nonindustrial diamonds, worked, but not mounted or set	161,600	Free
2620.90.50 Slag over 40% titanium*	140,300	Free
2901.29.50 Unsaturated acyclic hydrocarbons	77,157	Free
2614.00.60 Titanium ores and concentrates, not synthetic rutile	58,581	Free
7110.29.00 Palladium, in semimanufactured forms	54,920	Free
7110.41.00 Iridium, osmium and ruthenium, unwrought or powder form	34,712	Free
2844.10.20 Natural uranium compounds	30,738	Free
7601.10.60 Aluminum (other than alloy), unwrought	27,394	Free
8704.10.50 Motor vehicles: dumpers designed for off-highway use	27,350	Free
Duty-Free for All GSP Countries (5.9% of Top 25 Products)	**187,966**	
7606.12.30 Aluminum alloy, plates/sheets/strip	56,294	3.0%
7202.41.00 Ferrochromium containing more than 4 percent of carbon	42,932	1.9%
7202.30.00 Ferrosilicon manganese	37,400	3.9%
2804.69.10 Silicon, 99-99.99 percent silicon	29,086	5.3%
8708.70.45 Parts & Accessories of motor vehicles	22,254	2.5%
Duty-Free for LDC GSP Countries (9.7% of Top 25 Products)	**309,011**	
8703.24.00 Motor cars & other vehicles	255,632	2.5%
7202.11.50 Ferromanganese containing more than 4 percent of carbon	31,910	1.5%
7207.12.00 Iron or nonalloy steel semifinished products	21,469	0.8%
Duty-Free Only for AGOA Countries (0% of Top 25 Products)	**0**	
Textile & Apparel (2.7% of Top 25 Products)	**84,879**	
6110.20.20 Sweaters etc. of cotton	61,358	17.3%
6203.42.40 Men's or boys' trousers etc. of cotton	23,521	16.8%
Special (3.4% of Top 25 Products)	**109,155**	
9801.00.10 US goods returned	109,155	
Subtotal (Top 25 Products Account for 71.9% of Total)	3,182,859	
All Other	1,246,680	
Total	4,429,539	

Table A-42. Top 6 US imports from Sudan, 2001

Actual dollars, customs value, imports for consumption

HTS Item and Description	Imports	NTR Tariff
Duty-Free on NTR Basis (98.8% of top 6 products)	**3,344,359**	
1301.20.00 Gum Arabic	2,889,040	Free
1301.90.90 Natural gums, resins, gum-resins etc.	440,700	Free
8471.80.10 Control units for automatic data processing machines	7,538	Free
1207.40.00 Sesame seeds, whether or not broken	7,081	Free
Duty-Free For All GSP Countries (0.05% of top 6 products)	**1,690**	
4203.30.00 Belts and bandoliers of leather or of composition leather	1,690	2.7%
Duty-Free For LDC GSP Countries (0% of top 6 products)	**0**	
Duty-Free Only For AGOA Countries (0% of top 6 products)	**0**	
Textile & Apparel (0% of top 6 products)	**0**	
Special (1.2% of top 6 products)	**39,340**	
9801.00.10 US goods returned	39,340	
Subtotal (Top 6 Products Account 100% of Total)	3,385,389	
All Other	0	
Total	3,385,389	

Table A-43. Top 25 US imports from Swaziland, 2001

Actual dollars, customs value, imports for consumption

HTS Item and Description	Imports	NTR Tariff
Duty-Free on NTR Basis (14.2% of top 25 products)	**8,973,244**	
9403.60.80 Furniture of wooden	3,348,931	Free
4703.11.00 Chemical woodpulp etc. of unbleached coniferous wood	2,357,319	Free
8422.20.00 Machinery for cleaning or drying bottles etc.	1,689,956	Free
3406.00.00 Candles, tapers	690,946	Free
8441.30.00 Machines for making cartons, boxes, cases etc.	370,000	Free
9401.69.80 Seats with wooden frames, not upholstered	339,131	Free
9401.69.60 Chairs with wooden frames not upholstered	176,961	Free
Duty-Free For All GSP Countries (10.0% of top 25 products)	**6,369,003**	
1701.11.10 Cane sugar, raw, in solid form	6,369,003	[Complex]
Duty-Free For LDC GSP Countries (0.3% of top 25 products)	**168,216**	
2008.30.70 Grapefruit (other than peel or pulp)	168,216	1.1¢/kg.
Duty-Free Only For AGOA Countries (0% of top 25 products)	**0**	
Textile & Apparel (74.9% of top 25 products)	**47,495,908**	
6110.20.20 Sweaters etc. of cotton	23,514,652	17.3%
6105.10.00 Men's or boys' shirts, of cotton	6,747,937	20.0%
6203.42.40 Men's or boys' trousers and shorts of cotton	3,203,234	16.8%
6106.10.00 Women's or girls' blouses and shirts of cotton	3,083,010	20.0%
6204.62.40 Women's or girls' trousers etc. of cotton	2,741,391	16.8%
6110.30.30 Sweaters of manmade fibers	1,844,740	32.4%
6103.42.10 Men's or boys' trousers etc. of cotton	1,809,700	16.3%
6109.10.00 T-shirts, singlets etc. of cotton	1,245,600	17.4%
6104.62.20 Women's or girls' trousers etc. of cotton	1,136,404	15.3%
6105.20.20 Men's or boys' shirts, of manmade fibers	676,688	32.5%
6114.20.00 Garments of cotton	646,736	10.9%
6103.43.15 Men's or boys' trousers etc. of synthetic fibers	595,415	28.6%
6108.31.00 Women's or girls' nightdresses and pajamas of cotton	137,912	8.6%
6104.63.20 Women's or girls' trousers etc. of synthetic fibers	112,489	28.6%
Special (0.3% of top 25 products)	**214,220**	
9999.95.00 Informal entries under $1251	214,220	
Dutiable, No Preferences (0.3% of top 25 products)	**159,606**	
1701.99.50 Cane/beet sugar & pure sucrose, refined, in solid form	159,606	35.74¢/kg.
Subtotal (Top 25 Products Account for 97.5% of Total)	63,380,197	
All Other	1,655,814	
Total	65,036,011	

Table A-44. Top 25 US imports from Tanzania, 2001

Actual dollars, customs value, imports for consumption

HTS Item and Description	Imports	NTR Tariff
Duty-Free on NTR Basis (88.8% of top 25 products)	**23,407,863**	
7103.99.10 Precious or semiprecious stones for jewelry manufacture	10,273,535	Free
0304.20.60 Frozen fillets of fresh-water fish, flat fish, etc.	4,782,324	Free
1302.14.00 Saps and extracts of pyrethrum etc.	2,386,400	Free
0901.11.00 Coffee, not roasted, not decaffeinated	1,711,113	Free
7103.10.20 Precious stones & semiprecious stones, unworked	938,094	Free
1212.20.00 Seaweeds and other algae	797,307	Free
0801.32.00 Cashew nuts, fresh or dried, shelled	673,106	Free
0106.00.50 Live animals other than horses, asses, mules etc.*	346,995	Free
8525.20.30 Transceivers for radiotelephony etc.	237,112	Free
7102.31.00 Nonindustrial diamonds, unworked	207,990	Free
8428.60.00 Teleferics, chair lifts; traction mechanisms for funiculars	200,000	Free
4407.99.00 Nonconiferous woods sawn etc. over 6 mm thick	193,999	Free
1521.90.40 Insect waxes and spermaceti	162,050	Free
9705.00.00 Collections and collectors' pieces of zoological etc.	115,790	Free
0301.10.00 Live ornamental fish	103,994	Free
0902.40.00 Black tea (fermented) and partly fermented tea	103,594	Free
4103.90.00 Raw hides and skins of animals*	88,860	Free
7103.91.00 Rubies, sapphires and emeralds, worked	85,600	Free
Duty-Free For All GSP Countries (1.4% of top 25 products)	**373,231**	
4420.10.00 Wooden statuettes and other wood ornaments	191,051	3.2%
0106.00.10 Live birds, other than poultry*	182,180	1.8%
Duty-Free For LDC GSP Countries (3.0% of top 25 products)	**777,723**	
2401.20.83 Tobacco, partly or wholly stemmed/stripped	406,603	37.5¢/kg.
2401.20.85 Tobacco, partly or wholly stemmed/stripped	371,120	37.5¢/kg.
Duty-Free Only For AGOA Countries (0% of top 25 products)	**0**	
Textile & Apparel (1.4% of top 25 products)	**376,224**	
5209.11.00 Unbleached plain weave fabrics of cotton	376,224	6.5%
Special (5.4% of top 25 products)	**1,415,659**	
9999.95.00 Informal entries under $1251	770,641	
9801.00.10 US goods returned	645,018	
Subtotal (Top 25 Products Account for 96.8% of Total)	26,350,700	
All Other	878,507	
Total	27,229,207	

* : Product for which the 2002 version of the HTS uses a somewhat different classification than was used in 2001.

Table A-45. Top 25 US imports from Togo, 2001

Actual dollars, customs value, imports for consumption

HTS Item and Description	Imports	NTR Tariff
Duty-Free on NTR Basis (45.1% of top 25 products)	**5,668,551**	
3105.90.00 Mineral or chemical fertilizers	4,567,856	Free
0106.00.50 Live animals other than horses, asses, mules etc.*	571,855	Free
2302.30.00 Bran etc. from the sifting, milling of wheat	220,072	Free
0901.11.00 Coffee, not roasted, not decaffeinated	215,979	Free
1211.90.80 Plants and parts of plants used in perfumery, pharmacy etc.*	71,726	Free
9401.80.60 Seats other than of wood or with metal frame etc.	7,933	Free
0507.90.00 Tortoise shell etc. unworked; waste and powder	6,880	Free
9705.00.00 Collections and collectors' pieces of zoological etc.	3,950	Free
8471.49.70 Power supplies for computer	2,300	Free
Duty-Free For All GSP Countries (1.4% of top 25 products)	**177,755**	
2008.99.90 Fruit and other edible parts of plants	144,636	6.0%
4420.10.00 Wooden statuettes and other wood ornaments	8,576	3.2%
0713.33.40 Dried kidney beans, shelled, Sept. 1 - April 30	8,314	1.5¢/kg.
0710.80.70 Vegetables, frozen, not reduced in size	6,480	11.3%
7113.11.20 Silver articles of jewelry valued not over $18/dozen pieces	5,060	13.5%
6914.90.80 Ceramic (other than porcelain or china) articles	2,605	5.6%
4421.90.98 Articles of wood*	2,084	3.3%
Duty-Free For LDC GSP Countries (30.4% of top 25 products)	**3,818,875**	
2710.00.05 Distillate and residual fuel oils from bitum.mins.*	3,818,875	5.25¢/bbl.
Duty-Free Only For AGOA Countries (0% of top 25 products)	**0**	
Textile & Apparel (4.1% of top 25 products)	**519,592**	
6704.19.00 Wigs (partial) etc. of synthetic textile materials	261,859	Free
6704.11.00 Wigs (complete) of synthetic textile materials	223,596	Free
6703.00.30 Human hair, dressed etc. for use in making wigs	19,200	Free
6704.20.00 Wigs, false beards etc. of human hair	12,864	Free
6204.42.30 Women's or girls' dresses of cotton	1,073	9.2%
6214.90.00 Shawls etc. of textile materials	1,000	11.3%
Special (19.0% of top 25 products)	**2,396,207**	
9801.00.10 US goods returned	2,321,849	
9999.95.00 Informal entries under $1251	74,358	
Subtotal (Top 25 Products Account for 99.9% of Total)	12,580,980	
All Other	1,839	
Total	12,582,819	

* : Product for which the 2002 version of the HTS uses a somewhat different classification than was used in 2001.

Table A-46. Top 25 US imports from Uganda, 2001

Actual dollars, customs value, imports for consumption

HTS Item and Description	Imports	NTR Tariff
Duty-Free on NTR Basis (97.1% of top 25 products)	**17,294,511**	
0901.11.00 Coffee, not roasted, not decaffeinated	7,016,440	Free
0905.00.00 Vanilla beans	5,083,049	Free
0304.10.40 Fillets etc. fresh or chilled	2,160,688	Free
8105.10.60 Cobalt (other than alloy), unwrought*	1,365,744	Free
0304.20.60 Frozen fillets of fresh-water fish, flat fish, etc.	714,695	Free
1302.14.00 Saps and extracts of pyrethrum etc.	265,485	Free
0303.79.40 Fish, frozen	263,381	Free
2611.00.30 Tungsten ores	128,771	Free
0106.00.50 Live animals other than horses, asses, mules etc.*	82,829	Free
0304.20.20 Frozen fish fillets, skinned	63,600	Free
9706.00.00 Antiques of an age exceeding one hundred years	40,823	Free
0901.12.00 Coffee, not roasted, decaffeinated	35,226	Free
3507.90.70 Enzymes and prepared enzymes	24,375	Free
0302.69.20 Smelts, cusk, hake, etc.	13,284	Free
0302.32.00 Yellowfin tunas	11,065	Free
9601.10.00 Ivory, worked and articles	10,000	Free
1302.19.90 Vegetable saps and extracts	8,000	Free
8542.13.80 Monolithic digital integrated circuits*	7,056	Free
Duty-Free For All GSP Countries (1.7% of top 25 products)	**296,630**	
2611.00.60 Tungsten concentrates	157,429	[Complex]
8101.99.00 Tungsten, articles	114,129	3.7%
4420.10.00 Wooden statuettes and other wood ornaments	12,820	3.2%
4602.10.18 Baskets and bags of vegetable material	12,252	4.5%
Duty-Free For LDC GSP Countries (0% of top 25 products)	**0**	
Duty-Free Only For AGOA Countries (0% of top 25 products)	**0**	
Textile & Apparel (0.07% of top 25 products)	**12,975**	
6204.49.50 Women's or girls' dresses of textile materials	12,975	7.0%
Special (1.2% of top 25 products)	**205,829**	
9801.00.10 US goods returned	140,801	
9999.95.00 Informal entries under $1251	65,028	
Subtotal (Top 25 Products Account for 99.9% of Total)	17,809,945	
All Other	25,407	
Total	17,835,352	

* : Product for which the 2002 version of the HTS uses a somewhat different classification than was used in 2001.

Table A-47. Top 25 US imports from Zambia, 2001

Actual dollars, customs value, imports for consumption

HTS Item and Description	Imports	NTR Tariff
Duty-Free on NTR Basis (87.0% of top 25 products)	**13,540,250**	
8105.10.60 Cobalt (other than alloy), unwrought*	10,526,761	Free
7103.91.00 Rubies, sapphires and emeralds, worked	1,416,173	Free
4407.10.00 Coniferous wood sawn etc., over 6 mm thick	548,333	Free
0901.11.00 Coffee, not roasted, not decaffeinated	408,442	Free
7103.10.20 Precious stones & semiprecious stones, unworked	229,689	Free
7102.31.00 Nonindustrial diamonds, unworked	181,625	Free
0301.10.00 Live ornamental fish	165,022	Free
4407.91.00 Oak wood, saw etc. over 6 mm thick	30,377	Free
7103.99.10 Precious or semiprecious stones for jewelry manufacture	27,456	Free
9403.60.80 Furniture of wooden	6,372	Free
Duty-Free For All GSP Countries (7.2% of top 25 products)	**1,112,395**	
4418.90.40 Builders' joinery and carpentry of wood*	393,522	3.2%
4418.20.80 Doors of wood, other than French doors	246,458	4.8%
4107.29.60 Reptile leather, fancy*	238,640	2.4%
1209.99.40 Seeds, fruits and spores, of a kind used for sowing	114,600	0.83¢/kg.
0708.10.20 Peas, July 1 to Sept. 30	50,550	0.5¢/kg.
0708.10.40 Peas, Nov. 1 to June 30	24,909	2.8¢/kg.
4420.10.00 Wooden statuettes and other wood ornaments	19,667	3.2%
4602.10.18 Baskets and bags of vegetable material	17,799	4.5%
4202.31.30 Articles carried in the pocket or handbag of reptile leather	6,250	3.7%
Duty-Free For LDC GSP Countries (0.2% of top 25 products)	**28,679**	
0409.00.00 Natural honey	23,479	1.9¢/kg.
0708.90.40 Leguminous vegetables	5,200	4.9¢/kg.
Duty-Free Only For AGOA Countries (1.1% of top 25 products)	**174,193**	
0603.10.60 Roses, fresh cut	174,193	6.8%
Textile & Apparel (1.4% of top 25 products)	**217,980**	
6203.42.40 Men's or boys' trousers and shorts of cotton	217,980	16.8%
Special (3.1% of top 25 products)	**481,268**	
9801.00.10 US goods returned	468,767	
9999.95.00 Informal entries under $1251	12,501	
Subtotal (Top 25 Products Account for 99.8% of Total)	15,554,765	
All Other	29,545	
Total	15,584,310	

* : Product for which the 2002 version of the HTS uses a somewhat different classification than was used in 2001.

Table A-48. Top 25 US imports from Zimbabwe, 2001

Actual dollars, customs value, imports for consumption

HTS Item and Description	Imports	NTR Tariff
Duty-Free on NTR Basis (12.8% of top 25 products)	**10,253,842**	
7502.10.00 Nickel (other than alloy), unwrought	5,592,787	Free
9703.00.00 Original sculptures and statuary, in any material	2,051,385	Free
2516.11.00 Granite, crude or roughly trimmed	675,105	Free
0901.11.00 Coffee, not roasted, not decaffeinated	669,710	Free
2401.30.33 Tobacco refuse, from other tobacco, for cigarettes	662,531	Free
7112.90.00 Precious metal other than gold & platinum, waste and scrap*	602,324	Free
Duty-Free For All GSP Countries (52.4% of top 25 products)	**42,058,425**	
7202.41.00 Ferrochromium; weight more than 4 percent of carbon	14,890,456	1.9%
7113.19.10 Precious metal rope, curb for jewelry manufacture	8,324,686	7.0%
1701.11.10 Cane sugar, raw, in solid form	4,809,243	[Complex]
4107.90.60 Leather of animals, without hair on, fancy*	3,097,732	2.4%
4418.20.80 Doors of wood, other than French doors	2,644,583	4.8%
7113.19.29 Gold necklaces and neck chains (other than of rope)	1,790,335	5.5%
7113.19.21 Gold rope necklaces and neck chains	1,240,837	5.0%
2516.90.00 Porphyry, basalt and other monumental/building stone	1,232,423	3.0%
7113.19.50 Precious metal (other than silver) articles of jewelry	937,160	5.5%
6802.99.00 Monumental or building stone	884,097	6.5%
0712.90.80 Dried vegetables and mixtures of dried vegetables*	825,118	8.3%
0904.20.20 Paprika, dried or crushed or ground	752,870	3.0¢/kg.
6802.93.00 Monumental or building stone & articles of granite	628,885	3.7%
Duty-Free For LDC GSP Countries (17.5% of top 25 products)	**14,062,126**	
2401.20.85 Tobacco, partly or wholly stemmed/stripped	11,935,698	37.5¢/kg.
2401.20.83 Tobacco, partly or wholly stemmed/stripped	2,126,428	37.5¢/kg.
Duty-Free Only For AGOA Countries (0% of top 25 products)	**0**	
Textile & Apparel (17.3% of top 25 products)	**13,872,848**	
6203.42.40 Men's or boys' trousers and shorts of cotton	9,863,887	16.8%
6204.62.40 Women's or girls' trousers etc. of cotton	1,980,488	16.8%
6205.20.20 Men's or boys' shirts of cotton	1,062,590	20.0%
6204.52.20 Women's or girls' skirts etc. of cotton	965,883	8.3%
Special (0% of top 25 products)	**0**	
Subtotal (Top 25 Products Account for 88.6% of Total)	80,247,241	
All Other	10,312,560	
Total	90,559,801	

* : Product for which the 2002 version of the HTS uses a somewhat different classification than was used in 2001.